The Colours of...

'No longer just a thin layer of change,

but something that genuinely alters perception.'

Rem Koolhaas

Library of Congress Cataloging-in-Publication data. A CIP catalog record for this book has been applied for at the Library of Congress.

Bibliographic information published by the German National Library. The German National Library lists this publication in the Deutsche Nationalbibliografie; detailed bibliographic data are available on the Internet at http://dnb.dnb.de.

This publication is also available as an e-book (ISBN PDF 978-3-03821-365-9; ISBN EPUB 978-3-03821-685-8).

© 2015 VK Projects Naarden
© 2015 Birkhäuser Verlag GmbH, Basel
P.O. Box 44, 4009 Basel, Switzerland
Part of Walter de Gruyter GmbH,
Berlin/Munich/Boston

Printed on acid-free paper produced from chlorine-free pulp. TCF ∞

ISBN 978-3-03821-586-8

9 8 7 6 5 4 3 2 1

www.birkhauser.com

The Colours of...

Frank O. Gehry

Jean Nouvel

Wang Shu

BIG

Stefano Boeri

Zaha Hadid

Herzog & de Meuron

Steven Holl Architects

Toyo Ito

Lui Jiakun

Michael Malzan Architecture

Giancarlo Mazzanti

Enric Ruiz-Geli, Cloud 9

SANAA

Edited by

Cees W. de Jong

Essays by

Erik Mattie

Sophie Roulet

Bert de Muynck

Contents

'Colour reflects the turbulence that rocks societies around the world we live in.'

The Colours of...
Introduction by Cees W. de Jong

'That man came. Newton, with the help of nothing more than a prism, opened our eyes to the fact that light is an agglomeration of coloured rays which, all together, produce the colour white. (…) The first is the colour of fire; the second, lemon; the third, yellow; the fourth, green; the fifth, blue; the sixth, indigo; the seventh, violet. Each of these rays, though sifted afterwards through a hundred other prisms, will keep its colour unchanged, just as gold once refined changes no more in crucibles.' [1]

[1] Voltaire, Lettres philosophiques (1733) in: *Philosophical Letters: Letters Concerning the English Nation*. Dover Publications, Mineola, New York, 2003 (unabridged reprint of the Bobbs-Merrill, Indianapolis, Indiana, 1962 edition translated by Ernest Dilworth), p. 76.

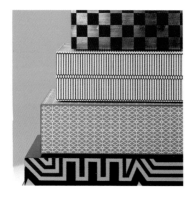

Alessandro Mendini.
Blue Galla Placidia.

Norman Foster.
'295 Yellow is the corporate colour
of the Renault Centre, Swindon, UK.
In turn, this building was an important
symbol of their corporate culture.'

'Colour has often been
considered the feminine
element in architecture,
which changes accord-
ing to fashion, rather
than which is eternal
and lasts.'

Rem Koolhaas.
Attribute. Personal choice red.
Hand-painted sample with brush strokes.
Colour red of BiC ballpoint.

Richard Meier.
White.

Colour is important to our lives, perhaps even essential. Artists, designers

and architects all use colour in their own unique and intensely personal

way. Colour reflects the turbulence that rocks societies around the world

we live in.

Our own personal connection to colour can also be a source of inspira-

tion. In the past I worked with four renowned architects, Mendini, Foster,

Koolhaas and Meier, to create and publish four completely different

books about colour. Each of these four architects has their own approach

to using colour:

'I have always treated the matter of colour in a very instinctive way. I may

rely on rules and methodologies, but they spring from instinct, not from

optico-scientific or spiritualistic facts.' *Alessandro Mendini* [2]

[2] In a conversation with Stefano Casciani, Italy. *Alessandro Mendini, 30 Colours*. Published in 1996, V+K Bussum / AkzoNobel.

'Colour is perceived with the eyes. Therefore, it is one of the elements

of reaction to the five senses, like flavour, taste, sound, smell ... Colour

might be like taste, or a kind of olfaction, a sort of sound. Indeed there

are similarities. There is something slightly culinary about putting colours together in a building, in an object, don't you think? And similarly, it is a rhythmic thing. In theories of colour, in fact, colour is repeatedly said to correspond to tones, sounds.' *Alessandro Mendini* [2]

'Historically, there is a long tradition of a distinction between the formal, or structural elements in architecture or painting and the element of colour (often represented as decorative or ornamental), between *disegno* and *colore*. This idea, which originates in Classical Greece, was redefined in the Renaissance and continues, through 19th century academic art theories like that of Charles Blanc, to the modern period. In my architecture also, colour seems generally to be distinct from those elements that form or shape a building: the structural members and the partitions or walls which delimit the space, although the yellow-painted structural frames of the Renault Centre seem to have been an important exception. Colour has often been considered the feminine element in architecture, which changes according to fashion, rather than which is eternal and lasts. Form and structure, on the other hand, have traditionally been perceived as masculine and enduring. In a world of shifting ideas about gender and its stereotypes, colour today plays a different role from the recent past in this respect.' *Norman Foster* [3]

'The modernist artist and designer László Moholy-Nagy claimed that what was most important in modern art, architecture and design was very often what was left out. In Foster's buildings, colour is not so much that which is left out, as the indeterminate element that connotes change and use within architecture, its sustainability, an element that is sometimes

[3] In a conversation between Norman Foster, John Small, Cees W. de Jong, Hans Ultee and Paul Overy at the offices of Sir Norman Foster and Partners at Riverside Three, 22 Hester Road, London SW11, on 27 June 1997. Norman Foster 30 Colours. Published in 1998, V+K Blaricum / AkzoNobel.

The Colours of...

introduced by the client. The client, that is to say, not in the traditional sense of the building's commissioner, but the person who uses it every day. Colour is the human element in Foster's architecture, but it is also the element of nature as opposed to the culture of materials and structure. And sometimes, colour is as much implied as applied.' *Paul Overy* in conversation with *Norman Foster* [3]

'There are two kinds of colours: ones that are integral to a material or a substance and cannot be changed, and ones that are artificial, that can be applied and that transform the appearance of things. This is the difference between colour and paint.' *Rem Koolhaas*

'White is the ephemeral emblem of perpetual movement.'

'White is the ephemeral emblem of perpetual movement. The white is always present but never the same – bright and rolling in the day, silver and effervescent under the full moon of New Year's Eve. Between the sea of consciousness and earth's vast materiality lies this ever-changing line of white. White is the light, the medium of understanding and transformative power.' *Richard Meier* [4]

[4] *Richard Meier. Thirty Colours.* Published in 2003, V+K Blaricum / AkzoNobel.

This new book, is inspired by a study of projects by *Frank O. Gehry, Jean Nouvel* and *Wang Shu*, architects who have totally different fundamental principles and who consistently produce surprising work. The creative process comprises a myriad of decisions, often based on long traditions and extensive research, that subsequently lead to unexpected outcomes.

The 'Swiss Army Knife', in bright red, is immediately recognisable around the world. It is a design icon, convenient and practical, and multifunctional and useful in a wealth of situations, whether on a survival expedition in the most remote corner of the earth, or at home or in the office to peel an apple for lunch or to use as a screwdriver. There are similarities between the 'Swiss Army Knife' and colour. For many designers and architects it is likewise a multifunctional medium.

In this book, I once again invite the architects of the projects to voice their opinions on colour in architecture:

'They are designed to encourage young musicians, their mentors and their audiences to try new things, to interact in new ways and to remain open to new experiences.' *Frank O. Gehry*

'The design for the 2010 Pavilion is a contrast of lightweight materials and dramatic, cantilevered, metal structures. The entire design is rendered in a vivid red that, in a play of opposites, contrasts with the green of its park setting. The colour reflects the iconic British images of traditional telephone boxes, post boxes and London buses.' *Jean Nouvel*

'A 45-metre-high rectangular box with transparent blue "screen" walls, the colour of the building changes constantly depending on the lighting conditions and time of day, both revealing and concealing the interior. At night the building lights up with images projected onto the "screen".' *Jean Nouvel*

'The campus is more similar to a traditional Chinese garden: when just finished it is not at its best. You have to wait, maybe even ten years, to let it grow and develop. My architecture needs time to change. In the beginning it is like a small chicken without feathers. Or like wine, or tea… it needs time.' *Wang Shu*

'This old and beautiful material is very cheap. This is how I convinced my client. Usually my budgets are very low, so that makes it interesting for them. In China, we are faced with an odd situation: mechanised building is very expensive, building manually is significantly cheaper.' *Wang Shu* [5]

[5] From an interview with Wang Shu conducted by Bert de Muynck / MovingCities on May 25, 2012.

The book profiles the work of these three architects, and their use of colour, using projects by each of the architects:

Frank O. Gehry

– Collage of form and colour: Museum of Biodiversity, Panama.

– Bend and fold colour: New World Symphony, Miami.

– Colour of the mind: Lou Ruvo Center for Brain Health, Las Vegas.

Jean Nouvel

– Coloured depths: Agbar Tower, Barcelona.

– Vivid red colour: Serpentine Pavilion, London.

– Lantern magic: Concert Hall, Copenhagen.

– A vibrant red line: The red kilometer, Bergamo

Wang Shu

– Old and beautiful material: Historic Museum, Ningbo.

– Traditional Chinese garden: Park Pavilion, Jinhua.

'The colour reflects the iconic British images of traditional telephone boxes, post boxes and London buses.'

- Architecture needs time to change: China Academy of Art, Hangzhou.

- Meditation and poetry: Wa Shan Guesthouse, Hangzhou

In addition, the book also contains projects by a series of architects whose work is based on totally different concepts and basic assumptions and that has produced some very interesting results.

BIG

- Light blue texture: Danish Pavilion, EXPO 2012, Shanghai.

- Colour-coded master plan: Superkilen Urban Park, Copenhagen.

Stefano Boeri

- Glass and basalt prism: Complex of Buildings at La Maddalena, Sardinia.

Zaha Hadid

- Suspended black: MAXXI Museum, Rome.

Herzog & de Meuron

- Many shades of green: 28 Condominiums at 40 Bond Street, New York.

Steven Holl Architects

- Open colour: Linked Hybrid Apartment Complex, Beijing.

Toyo Ito

- Polished painted colour: Mihimoto Ginza 2, Tokyo.

Lui Jiakun

- Favourite colour pink: Hu Huishan Earthquake Memorial, Sichuan.

Michael Malzan Architecture

- Rhythm of light and shadow: New Carver Apartments, Los Angeles.

- Texture, form, light and colour: Inner City Arts Campus, Los Angeles.

Giancarlo Mazzanti

– Interrelated colour: Timayui School, Santa Marta.

Enric Ruiz-Geli, Cloud 9

– Transparent colour: Media Tic Building, Barcelona.

SANAA

– Bright golden colour: Derek Lam Store, New York.

'The pavilion is a monolithic structure in white painted steel which keeps it cool during hot Shanghai summers due to its heat-reflecting character-istics. The roof is covered with a light blue surface texture, the same as that used for Danish cycle paths.' *BIG*

'The master plan for the park, stretching approximately one kilometre from Nørrebrogade to Tagensvej, has been divided into three areas, each with a different colour to mark specific functions.' *BIG*

'A glass cube suspended over the water – the Conference Hall, the most representative of the interventions, is a glass and basalt prism that canti-levers over the water.' *Stefano Boeri*

'Entering the atrium, the main elements of the project are evident: con-crete curved walls, suspended black staircases, and an open ceiling that catches natural light. A new fluid kind of spatiality of multiple perspective points and fragmented geometry, designed to embody the chaotic fluid-ity of modern life.' *Zaha Hadid*

'The roof is covered with a light blue surface texture, the same as that used for Danish cycle paths.'

'The colour of the building is the colour of the glass, with its many shades of green, which depend on the light, viewing angle, thickness and the glass layering.' *Herzog & de Meuron*

'Filmic urban public space running around, over and through multi-faceted spatial layers, as well as the many passages that run through the project, make the Linked Hybrid an "open city within a city".' *Steven Holl*

'The interior is painted pink in memory of the girl's favourite colour.'

'The exterior is plastered in a dark grey similar to that of the makeshift tents, while the interior is painted pink in memory of the girl's favourite colour.' *Lui Jiakun*

'The tower is basically a rectangular box, and from a distance resembles a typical skyscraper. However, it is at its most appealing at night when different coloured lights make the irregular windows glow, revealing the glamorous interior of the building.' *Toyo Ito*

'This process was done by hand and required up to 6 different stages of polishing and painting to ensure the smooth finish required by the customer. The building has become a jewel in the Ginza district, with an exterior that shines in a pink tone like a pearl, its windows scattered across the facade like bubbles or dancing petals.' *Toyo Ito*

'A series of fins trace across the circular edge of the central space as it rises through the building, creating a rhythm of light and shadow across the gathering spaces below.' *Michael Malzan*

'Within, the space of the courtyard and the studios weave a texture of form, light, colour and learning to inspire and embrace the growth of the individual. The ceramics tower beckons as a symbol of the connections forged between students, the community and the world at large.'

Michael Malzan

'The module is designed as a flexible and neutral space that can accommodate the development of multiple activities within it. It relates to its immediate external surroundings and facilitates a close relationship between the children and the teachers.' *Giancarlo Mazzanti*

'A completely green Meccano model with randomly placed transparent bubbles, the Media-Tic was conceived as an incubator to establish links between state agencies and technology-media communications firms.'

Enric Ruiz-Geli, Cloud 9

'For the walls, the building's original brickwork was kept, but painted white; combined with the transparent central forms and the light reflecting on the walls and the acrylic, they make a subtle contrast to the store's concrete grey floor. Bright golden-coloured fabric screens can be drawn for extra privacy and special occasions.' *SANAA*

This book is a specifier of material, substance, light, texture, form and colour – and in the end of human emotion.

Frank O. Gehry

The balance between form and colour

By Erik Mattie

'Working with colour will always remain a journey, a search for a true understanding of the fundamental principles, the methodology and underlying philosophy. It is a quest into the wonderful world of architecture, the "mother of all fine arts"; painting and sculpture are among her children.' [1]

[1] Michelangelo (1475–1564)

Canadian American Frank O. Gehry (born Ephraim Owen Goldberg in 1929) is generally considered one of the greatest and most influential architects American post-war architecture has ever known.[2] From the sixties – when overly rigid modernism began to give rise to critical questions – until the present, Gehry has proven himself a trendsetter. One whose name is connected to nearly every post-war architectural movement there is: from postmodernism and philosophically inclined deconstructionism to expressionism. This harbours a paradox: his most important work is characterised by white wall surfaces, as white as those of pre-war modernists, the very same modernism Gehry's generation rebelled against so fervently. And the daring geometric planes, dissected and twisted blocks, cylinders and other geometric shapes are reminiscent of the avant-garde designs of the expressionists, deconstructionists and even the futurists of the 20th century, designs that were never realised.[3] But Gehry's architecture refuses to be placed in a single category. His oeuvre is much too complex and layered. Gehry's use of colour is largely determined by his choice of materials, and much less by colour swatches.

[2] From 2001, The Gehry Partnership, Gehry Partners, LLP.

[3] Jodidio 1993.

The combinations displayed in his buildings, between copious shapes and rectangular flat surfaces, plastered sheer white and natural stone or brick, experimental use of materials and a subtle yet expressive colour palette, have led Gehry to be considered perhaps more an artist than simply an architect. This is due in part to the architect's own ambivalent opinion in this respect, but is also the result of an exhibition at New York's MoMA, which launched the careers of Gehry and six other exciting architects. The exhibition, organised by Philip Johnson – who was also responsible for the ground-breaking architecture exhibition on the modernist International Style in 1932 in the same museum – did not so much aim to label a style movement, but brought the seven together in terms of their common daring, unparalleled intensity and sometimes confusing language of form.

Gehry was represented in the exhibition with relatively early work from the 1970s: two houses in Santa Monica (near Los Angeles), including his own home. The shapes and spaces seem to have been literally pulled apart, and the cheap materials he used, such as fencing and corrugated

4 Calvin Tomkins, 'Man of Steel', The New Yorker, 05/08/2002.

5 Brand, p. 184.

iron, add to the impression of foreignness that the unsuspecting passer-by experiences on seeing it. The three smaller houses built on a relatively small but long plot of land in Venice (California) were also designed by Gehry and are characterised by square, sculptural shapes and unexpected materials. Every house has a facade made of a different material, in a different colour: green bitumen shingles, multiplex and blue stucco. The first two materials are certainly inexpensive, but they were not chosen out of frugality. The objective is the experiment: in shape, form, material, texture and ultimately also in colour. The experiment is not limited to the building's exterior. Extraordinary shapes are also to be found in the interior and the furnishings. Examples include Gehry's corrugated cardboard furniture, including the well-known *Wiggle Side chair*, which has been added to the Vitra collection. Reference is often made to Gehry's youth, when his grandmother encouraged him to play with materials he could find in his grandfather's hardware store.[4] This explanation, while entertaining, is much too simplistic, and it is clear that Gehry's creativity knows few bounds. In this respect, the differences of opinion between Gehry and his good friend, the sculptor Richard Serra, are especially interesting. Gehry has invited Serra to participate in various projects and his monumental sculptures in corroded steel are an extraordinarily excellent match to Gehry's own choice of materials. Serra recognises that there is an overlap between a freely creative artist and an architect who designs a functional building for a client, but ultimately he considers them to be two separate disciplines. Gehry is inclined to make the pragmatic aspect of his profession submissive to the artistic will of form.[5]

Frank O. Gehry

It is telling that Gehry counts or counted not only Serra, but also other artists such as Robert Rauschenberg (1925-2008), Claes Oldenburg (1925) and Edward Kienholz (1927-1994) among his intimate friends. Rauschenberg, the sculptural painter, experimented with various unusual materials, while the other two sculptors have an extremely spatial perspective. Slightly more surprising is Gehry's comparison of his design for a guesthouse in Wayzata (Minnesota) to a *painting*, a still life by Morandi.[6]   [6] Papadakis.

Philip Johnson and many other architectural critics seem to give Gehry the benefit of the doubt: Gehry is an artist, a great artist. In 1983 he was awarded the Arnold W. Brunner Prize for his contribution to architecture as an art form, and in 1989 Gehry received the Pritzker prize for best architect.

After his humble beginnings as a 'deconstructionist', when Gehry predominantly designed more intimate houses, many larger assignments followed – in part due to his inclusion in the MoMA exhibition. From that time on, Gehry began to create a uniquely personal vernacular within the already striking language of form, a vernacular that is perhaps best described in rather graphic and associative terms as the billowing sails of a ship, and more prosaically as a harmony of opened and folded three-dimensional geometrical figures: sphere, block, pyramid, triangle and multigon.

The first building in which Gehry unfolded his concave and convex shapes was the renowned Vitra Design Museum in Weil am Rhein, not far from the similarly expressive – and equally white – chapel outside Ronchamp by Le Corbusier. This was also Gehry's first work outside of the US and the first building where he reduced the materials of the exterior to white plaster and greyish metal, in this case titanium-zinc. The colour accent comes instead from the sculpture placed directly alongside the building, Claes Oldenburg's *Balancing Tools*, painted red, white and blue in a landscape of green grass.

The sculptural composition is not only defined by the concave and convex shapes, but also by sharp block shapes, at times fused with the spheres and cylinders, sometimes featured separately. In the latter case, material and colour accentuate the differentiation of shape. The Weisman Art Museum in Minneapolis from 1993 is an orgy of bulging shapes, lined with stainless steel, while on the other side of the multi-sided building, the rectangular facade planes in orange-red bricks dominate the building's appearance. The American Center in Paris, now the Cinémathèque Française, from 1994 is equally exuberant in its convex and concave and angular shapes, but instead of metal, Gehry opted to use yellow sandstone, characteristic for Paris and the Île-de-France. The Guggenheim Museum Bilbao was opened in 1997 and made Gehry world famous, its spiralling shapes covered in titanium. The rectangular box seems to have been banished completely from this building, which is generally considered to be an iconic example of contemporary architecture. The Guggenheim firmly put the former provincial town on the map: the city and the museum have become inseparably linked.

In 2003, the Walt Disney Concert Hall was completed, the fourth hall of the Los Angeles Music Center, and the first large, classical music hall Gehry designed. Completion was much later than scheduled (the first

'The Guggenheim Museum Bilbao was opened in 1997 and made Gehry world famous, its spiralling shapes covered in titanium.'

design dated from 1991) and the hall came in at over three times the original budget. An interesting detail is that during the trouble-ridden construction of the building, the original red brick for the rolling facade was replaced by less expensive polished grey stainless steel in order to reduce costs. The acoustics of the hall (2265 seats), with a central podium for the Los Angeles Philharmonic Orchestra, are among the best in the world (which is not the only similarity between this hall and the hall of the Berliner Philharmonie by Hans Scharoun). The MARTa Herford Museum in Germany followed in 2005, and featured equally awe inspiring shapes, and – just like the Parisian design – did not incorporate polished grey metal but local materials: in this case, modest red brick. Despite the rather frequent application of local building materials, the real common denominator in Gehry's work, other than the formal composition of merging and fusing convex and concave spherical volumes in contrast with the sharp-edged rectangles of the functional facades, is the use of metal, usually titanium-zinc or stainless steel. Even in his earlier work, before the 'billowing sails', Gehry experimented with copper shapes covered in lead or zinc. The breakthrough for the general public came only after form and material became an inseparable entity. The wilder forms were given calmer colours that are more introverted and simple: greyish metal combined with white plaster. Here the dark grey of shadows lends the somewhat limited colour palette of the design extraordinary dynamism. The following pages elaborate on three of Gehry's later projects that do not only display the coming of age of this concept, but also its further growth by means of colour use. In the case of the

Lou Ruvo Center, a covered promenade becomes an intimate area, the colour use restrained in soft pastels, while the New World Symphony employs brightly coloured light that burns bright as a beacon, from the inside to the outside. In the Panama Museum of Biodiversity, the colours are as uncompromising as the shape of the roof, which consists of folded and pressed down sheets.

Lou Ruvo Center for Brain Health, Las Vegas, 2010

The Lou Ruvo Center for Brain Health was founded by Larry Ruvo in honour and memory of Lou Ruvo, Larry's deceased father who suffered from Alzheimer's disease. In order to raise awareness of this illness, Ruvo looked for and found the solution in establishing a new clinic, a clinic that would not only provide special care to patients and undertake every effort and means to promote (clinical) research into the disease, but would also be a clinic that would attract global attention due to its unique architecture. Ruvo felt that no one would be better suited to this task than Frank Gehry. After some hesitation, and only because Ruvo assented that the centre would also harbour patients suffering from Huntington's disease, a (brain) disease the effects of which Gehry had seen first hand, Gehry agreed. The result clearly reflects its creator. Concave and convex shapes, covered in stainless steel earn the building a place among the city's landmarks, eclipsing even its neighbour, the World Market Center, a 460,000 square metre large wholesale trade centre, 70 times larger than the clinic. The arched forms of the communal and activity areas are purely aesthetic.

'Concave and convex shapes, covered in stainless steel earn the building a place among the city's landmarks.'

Frank O. Gehry

The windows, that nod and follow the form of the arch, let in light but do not reflect the building layers. The actual care, research and administrative activities take place in the more conservatively designed rectangular spaces, the exteriors of which – in typical Gehry style – are also comprised of rectangular planes. The complex consists of two more or less independent buildings, separated by a semi-openable inner promenade. It is this intimate space that defies the harsh colour scheme of white and gray. Here, the colour planes are painted in soft pastels. The structural iron columns are also painted, which dissolves the differentiation between construction and walls in the larger entity of the composition.

New World Symphony, Miami Beach, 2011

The New World Symphony in Miami Beach, opened in 2011, is a true Gehry in every respect, although the exuberance – in the form of twisted cylinders and cubes – has been reserved for the interior. Gehry made a deliberate decision to keep the exterior simple due to the building's location in Art Deco dominated Miami. The white wall planes are an elegant contrast to the leafy surroundings, a landscape design by West 8. In the interior of the relatively small concert hall (756 seats) and the other public areas such as the foyer, Gehry has however succeeded brilliantly in equalling the overwhelming experience of the Guggenheim in Bilbao. Similar to the much larger Disney Concert Hall, the orchestra has been placed at the centre of the hall, creating a sense of intimacy. The concert hall is a testament to Gehry's mastery of light and colour. The initially monochromatic white convex surfaces of the hall's expressive design not

'The concert hall is a testament to Gehry's mastery of light and colour.'

only benefit the acoustics, but also serve as projection screens for colour schemes and other purposes. The foyer is also illuminated from the inside, albeit more subtly. And finally, the interior is visible from the outside, thanks to the glass fibre facade and the fact that one of the large white colour planes outside is an immense outdoor projection screen. For Gehry, light and colour merge completely in the concept of his design.

The driving force behind this building, not just the music hall, but also the orchestra education centre, was Michael Tilton Thomas (MTT), founder and director of the orchestra and an old acquaintance of Gehry's. In the fifties, the architecture student was the future musician's babysitter. Whether as an architect or sculptor, Gehry is a harmonious artist in all respects.

Panama Museum of Biodiversity, 2014

The history of this design dates back to 1999, the year in which ownership of the Panama Canal was transferred to the national authorities. However, it took until 2002 for the assignment to be given the green light. Construction was problematic, not least due to the complexity of the roof structure. Despite the arduous process, the result was worth it. The museum, which displays the splendour of the nation's flora and fauna in an ecological context, exemplifies Gehry's bold layering of roof shapes that look like they have just suffered the onslaught of a tornado. This apparent disastrous force of nature has somehow left a bulky, block-shaped part of the building unscathed, manifesting the contrast between order and chaos, so very typical of Gehry's work. However, the form also reflects the origins of the country, where Panama sits between two oceans and

'It is as though the colour palette of the biodiversity of the tropics has had a profound influence on Gehry.'

Frank O. Gehry

two continents. Never before has Gehry designed such a bright and

colourful building. It is as though the colour palette of the biodiversity

of the tropics has had a profound influence on Gehry. Despite this bold

cacophony of colours, the concept of the museum is completely clear.

The *galleries*, the café, the gift shop and the two strips of greenery

designed by Bruce Mau all extend like rays of sunlight from a centrally

located atrium. Every part of the building, thematically ordered, can be

recognised and experienced by its form and colour.

This project also has a personal aspect to it: Berta Isabel Aquilera,

partner within LLP and Gehry's wife, is originally from Panama.

Nearly every project of Gehry's is iconic and establishes architecture as a

noble art form. However, there is also room for a minor point of criticism.

Gehry, revered as the father of the Los Angeles School (even he cannot

escape a style label), was one of the first to look for a way to address the

endless American post-war urban sprawl with its repetitive expanding

grids, its lack of a city centre, and its landscape dominated by traffic and

roadways.[7] By building his structures in green areas, he attempts to sof-

ten the transition from buildings to highway. Gehry's sculptural buildings

are visual landmarks and functional meeting points, and consequently

they become new centres and focal points for the wider area. However,

this concept is much more effective – and this is quite a statement – in

European cities than in the United States, where visitors tend to travel

only along the main roads. By default, American cities lack intimacy,

whereas Gehry's buildings are always intimate. The building is stronger

[7] Papadakis.

than its surroundings. However, the New World Symphony might just as well be in Las Vegas, just as the Lou Ruvo Center could be in Miami. And that, as is the case with all art, is the final paradox: there is no interaction between Gehry's buildings and their surroundings, although every one of his designs serves as a crown jewel to those same surroundings, an exceptional jewel and an icon of the city and its future.

'There is no interaction between Gehry's buildings and their surroundings.'

Reference literature

Brand, Jan: Janselijn, Han, *Architectuur en Verbeelding, Architecture and Imagination*. Waanders, Zwolle 1989.

Desmier-Maulion, Annick, *Paris, La couleur de la ville*. Éditions de La Villette. Paris 2002.

Jodidio, Philip, *Contemporary American Architects*. Taschen Verlag, Cologne 1993.

Jodidio, Philip, *New Forms: Architecture in the 1990s*. Taschen Verlag, Cologne 2001.

Papadakis, Andreas; Steele, James, *Architecture of Today*. Rizzoli Publications, New York 1997.

Taverne, Ed; Wagenaar, Cor, *The Color of the City*. V+K, Laren 1992.

This is the first building in Latin America by Frank Gehry. A team of experts from the Smithsonian Institute and the University of Panama developed the scientific content of the Panama Museum of Biodiversity. The conceptual design of the museum's galleries is the work of Bruce Mau Design. The museum offers the opportunity to discover the value of Panama's biodiversity and the educational programme will cater for 40,000 schoolchildren, free of charge, every year.

- Educate: Instruct visitors and the public about the importance of biodiversity.
- Network of exchanges: The museum will be a place where visitors can learn about the natural and cultural wealth of Panama.
- Convey: The museum aims to become a landmark with eight galleries. Eight 'devices of wonder', linking the emergence of the isthmus of Panama.

Frank O. Gehry
Collage of form and colour

 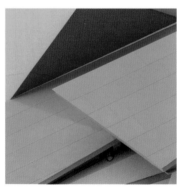

Frank O. Gehry

Museum of Biodiversity, Panama

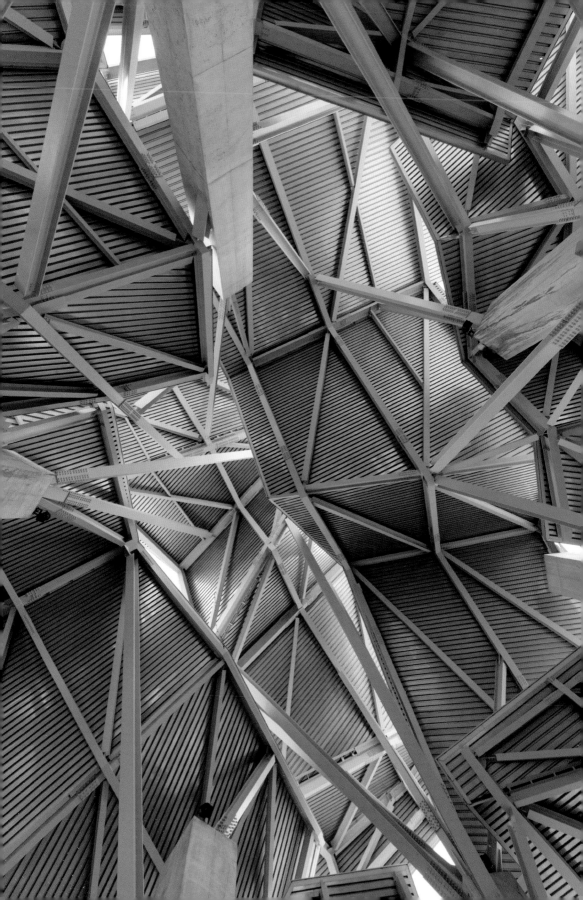

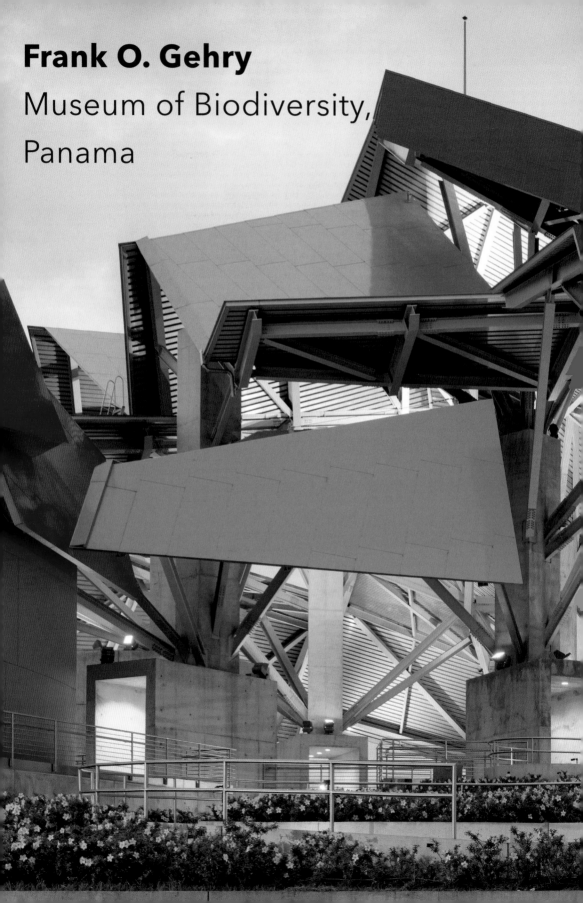

Frank O. Gehry
Museum of Biodiversity, Panama

Frank O. Gehry

Frank O. Gehry

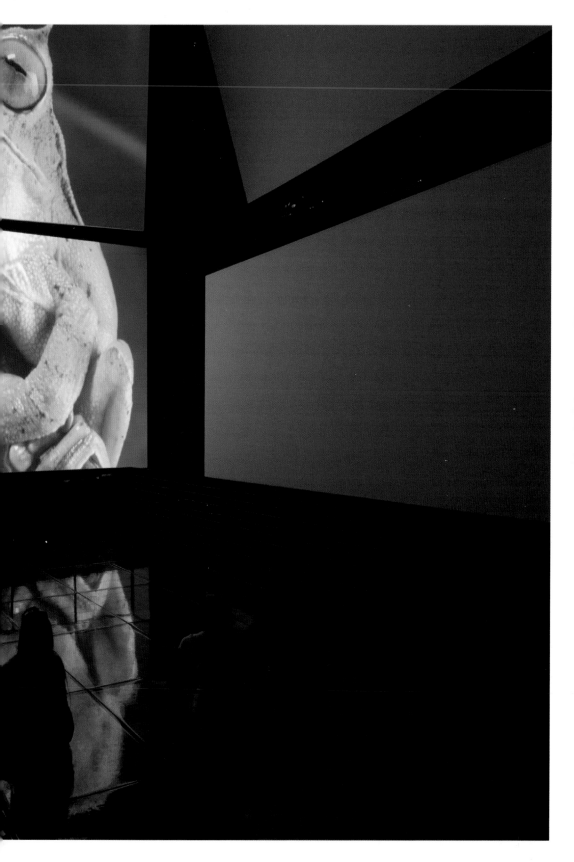

Museum of Biodiversity, Panama

Frank O. Gehry

Museum of Biodiversity, Panama

Museum of Biodiversity, Panama

This new facility in the centre of Miami Beach was designed by Frank Gehry in close collaboration with the New World Symphony's founder and artistic director Michael Tilson Thomas. The rectangular white building showcases Gehry's characteristic bends and folds on the interior, which are visible through the high, glass curtain-wall facade of the main entrance.

'Not only are we marking a new era for this organisation and giving our musicians an unrivalled facility in which to learn and achieve their potential, but we are also inviting everyone to experience classical music in a new kind of space, one that is designed to engage and to energise and that will move people from around the world to think about music in new ways.' *Michael Tilson Thomas.*

'I hope the spirit of creative engagement that Michael and I have enjoyed will live on in the building's spaces. They are designed to encourage young musicians, their mentors and their audiences to try new things, to interact in new ways and to remain open to new experiences.'

Frank O. Gehry
Bend and fold colour

Frank O. Gehry

New World Symphony, Miami

Frank O. Gehry

New World Symphony, Miami

Frank O. Gehry

New World Symphony, Miami

Frank O. Gehry

New World Symphony, Miami

Frank O. Gehry

New World Symphony, Miami

Frank O. Gehry
Colour of the mind

The Center operates as an outpatient treatment and research facility in downtown Las Vegas.

The Center includes examination rooms, offices for health care practitioners and researchers, a 'Museum of the Mind', a community auditorium and also serves as the headquarters for Keep Memory Alive, the Las Vegas Alzheimer's Association and the Las Vegas Parkinson's Disease Association. Keep Memory Alive was founded by Larry Ruvo and his wife Camille, in memory of his father, Lou Ruvo, a victim of Alzheimer's Disease, and is supported by the Ruvo Family and other participants.

Frank O. Gehry

Lou Ruvo Center for Brain Health, Las Vegas

Frank O. Gehry

Lou Ruvo Center for Brain Health,
Las Vegas

Lou Ruvo Center for Brain Health, Las Vegas

Frank O. Gehry

Lou Ruvo Center for Brain Health, Las Vegas

Frank O. Gehry

Frank O. Gehry

Lou Ruvo Center for Brain Health, Las Vegas

Jean Nouvel

Images in colour

By Sophie Roulet

'The primary question for this most modern architect of the day is therefore how well the essence can be represented by the connection between light and matter.'

Monochrome, diffracted, luminous and moving, the use of colour in Jean Nouvel's work is inseparable from the image – in every sense of the word – that his architecture refers to. Whether allegorical or symbolic, those images are as universal in the words he uses as they are in the buildings of this architect, an international star always dressed in black, brilliantly wielding colourful metaphors and paradoxes.

Refuting all kinds of style and contending that the future of architecture is not architectural in an era in which it is all about image, Nouvel was awarded the Pritzker Prize in 2008 at the age of 62. The jury saw it as a tribute to the taste for creative experimentation of an author whose production, in spite of globalisation, has in fact never become standardised or repetitive.

His buildings are full of images and evoke the sentiment that each new situation requires new architecture that adopts a standpoint in relation to its background. Splendid and coherent to some, contentious to others, this is the trademark of an architect known for his use of visual effects and colour. Contextual but also conceptual, his projects 'never ignore where they are nor what is situated around them,' says Nouvel, for whom concept is essential. In his jargon, he speaks 'about hyper-specificity' as the basis of his work. On the occasion of his retrospective exhibition at the Centre Pompidou in 2002, he explained how a pre-existing state becomes an excuse for him to draw, a way of facing the impossibility of inventing *ex nihilo*. Mulling over questions with his teams, Nouvel accumulates all kinds of ideas and images that become part of the synergy of creating a concept. Evoking the sensations, emotions and aspirations of the moment in his work, he considers himself to be an architect of the spirit of the time. Through the images, colours intersect and overlap in his architecture, which he himself defines as a backdrop.

'This is the trademark of an architect known for his use of visual effects and colour.'

In his constant search to express the singular poetics of place, colour is either intensified, the monumentality of black heightened by the stark introduction of red, or else tends towards an immateriality never quite fulfilled through the means of transparency, filters and mirrors.

By Sophie Roulet

Nouvel interrogates the questions of the modern world through the medium of light. Experimenting with material, tonality, shadows and light until the colours are saturated, Jean Nouvel constructs pathways, sequences and tracking shots as if in the movies. It is but one step from the image as an architectural concept to the materiality of colour.

The impact of red and black

Through his projects, Jean Nouvel develops a strong idea that can also be called a 'concept', which he continues to simplify until it condenses into an image. One such example is the technical headquarters of Brembo, a manufacturer of automotive brakes. Known as the 'kilometro rosso', its distinguishing feature is a wall of sheet steel with Ferrari-red lacquer, an immense billboard running for one kilometre along a stretch of the Milan-Venice motorway near Bergamo in Italy. Completed in 2007, this landmark defines a place through its strong visual impact, creating a barrier between the chaos of the motorway and the research centre hidden behind it and its natural surroundings. This structure, more than ten metres high, is fashioned from special aluminium profiles that highlight the brightness of its red colour, a tribute to the company that makes brakes for many Formula 1 teams, including Ferrari.

Prior to this daring use of bright red, Nouvel had already made headlines with the black anthracite of the Palais de Justice built in 2000 on the Île de Nantes in France, whose symbolism many considered too stark. Contrasting the red wood of the courtrooms, Nouvel coloured his building

'Nouvel interrogates the questions of the modern world through the medium of light.'

black to express the power and the strength of justice, while at the same time denoting its transparency – the other requirement of such an institution – through the inclusion of huge walls of glass.

In this 'black work', the words rigor, rigidity, rationality and transparency draw their meaning from the industrial past of this site. That sombre fortress of steel opened, however, onto a garden of ash trees in contrast to the 1500 tons of steel structure. The radical design of the law courts has been criticised for its "prison-like" aesthetics as well as its colour and monumentality, although Nouvel wrote at the time (Libération, 10 July 2000) that, 'Justice should express its power. There is nothing more terrible than pretending that justice is kind and insignificant. A courthouse that looks like a cultural centre is misleading the world. It's even suspicious on a democratic level. For me, architectural design isn't intended for consensus. Only buildings that are forgotten don't provoke debate.'

Another of Nouvel's buildings, this time a temporary structure, the 'Red Sun Pavilion' was created in 2010 as a symbol for London and intended to put the fire into Kensington Gardens. To 'catch the sun' on the occasion of the 10th anniversary of the Serpentine Gallery, Jean Nouvel elected to colour his first building on British soil red to capture a number of sensations related to the sun and to summer. 'That symphony of reds which vary throughout the day and the seasons contrasts with the green trees, echoing the famous phone boxes, letterboxes and buses in London,' he explained. Made entirely of glass, metal, textile membrane and polycarbonate, the audacious pavilion proclaimed itself loud and clear, appearing to defy gravity and shedding its roof of huge retractable awnings. For many, however, particularly those more accustomed to the light, and to the modesty of the previous annual pavilions, the Red Sun Pavilion was a form of 'terrorism'.

Polychrome landscape

For Jean Nouvel, there is no contradiction between architecture and a representative image whose vocabulary fits the project in the same way as colour. For the Museum of Primitive Arts which opened on the Quai Branly in Paris in 2006, the image becomes the description of a landscape in colour. Covered with exotic bark, the pillars that support those darkest shadows are reminiscent of a tropical forest, creating an initiatory territory designed to protect art works from abroad. In his letter of intent addressed to the international competition, the architect wrote in 1999: 'In a place inhabited by symbols of forests and rivers, by obsessions of death and oblivion, it is an asylum for censored and cast-off works from Australia and the Americas. [...] Away then, with the structures, mechanical systems, with curtain walls, with emergency staircases, parapets, false ceilings, projectors, pedestals, showcases… If their functions must be retained, they must disappear from our view and our consciousness. [...] In order to obtain this result [...], windows are very large and very transparent, and often printed with huge photographs.'

To make the material appear opaque, Jean Nouvel creates images and colours by means of a polychrome landscape. On Quai Branly, the green tones of a vegetal wall harmoniously complement the red tones of the boxes located on the north side. From the garden, the 'stage of greenery' designed by landscape architect Gilles Clément, the main facade of the museum is characterised by cubes of colour, in red hues, each dedicated to a specific culture. Between those cubes, a polychrome film representing the dense vegetation from tropical countries creates a stained glass effect within. Coloured thorns, geometrical patterns and three-coloured frescos composed of white, red and black complete the composition of an internal and external landscape. Saturated with narrative colours, the building evokes the symbols of life and nature that permeate primitive art. Through his use of colour, Jean Nouvel once again delivers his customary plethora of images and intentions.

Light matter

With the Agbar Tower, completed in 2005, colour became a veritable player in the city of Barcelona. The interaction with light adds a new dimension to the lone physical presence of this skyscraper, in the American sense. Jean Nouvel prefers to describe it as 'an emergence, rising singularly in the centre of a generally calm city'. An urban symbol, in much the same way as Gaudí's constructions, the Agbar Tower changes the shape of the landscape as a whole with its one hundred and forty-four metres. Aside from its original, tapered profile shape based on an egg-shaped plan, reminiscent of the Swiss Re Tower designed in

'On Quai Branly, the green tones of a vegetal wall harmoniously complement the red tones of the boxes located on the north side.'

By Sophie Roulet

London by Norman Foster, the tower consists of a sophisticated double skin concealing an array of variously textured and coloured materials. On the inside, the concrete core is covered with aluminium-coated shingles and on the outside, articulated glass strips diffract the sun's rays, giving the facade a sense of mysterious depth. Dressed in a palette of forty different shades, the fractal image of the Agbar Tower varies depending on the luminosity and angle of view. At night, its envelope transforms, illuminated by light-emitting diodes that interfere with the superimposition of three filters: the perforations in shimmering frames, cladding colours and glass strips. Designed by Alain Bony, the now-famous cladding is comprised of several thousand coloured plates. Their hues vary from red-brown to green and ochre in the lower part, mimicking the ambient colour of the buildings in Barcelona, gradually turning to blues and greys to become muted at the base of the glass cupola crowning the building.

'The perforations in shimmering frames, cladding colours and glass strips.'

For Jean Nouvel, it's about alluding to 'a fluid mass that bursts through the ground like a geyser under permanent, calculated pressure. The surface of the building evokes water: smooth and continuous, shimmering and transparent, its materials reveal themselves in nuanced shades of colour and light [...] to make the Agbar tower resonate against Barcelona's skyline.'

The primary question for this most modern architect of the day is therefore how well the essence can be represented by the connection between light and matter. By playing with depth of the field, with accelerating interferences and other illusions he brings about the de-

materialization of space. And by blurring our awareness of geometrical

notions he makes it possible to sense another materiality and its chro-

matic characteristics. With Jean Nouvel, colour unquestionably reveals its

spatial properties.

By Sophie Roulet

This is not a tower. It is not a skyscraper in the American sense of the expression: it is a unique growth in the middle of this rather calm city. But here it is not the slender, nervous verticality of the spires and bell towers that so often punctuate horizontal cities. Instead, it is a fluid mass that has perforated the ground – a geyser under a permanent calculated pressure.

The surface of this construction evokes the water: smooth and continuous, but also vibrating and transparent because it manifests itself in coloured depths – uncertain, luminous and nuanced. This architecture comes from the earth but does not have the weight of stone. It could even be the faraway echo of old formal Catalan obsessions, carried by a mysterious wind from the coast of Montserrat.

The uncertainties of matter and light make the campanile of Agbar vibrate in the skyline of Barcelona: a faraway mirage day and night; a precise marker to the entry of the new diagonal that starts at Plaça de les Glòries. This singular object becomes a new symbol for an international city.

Jean Nouvel
Coloured depths

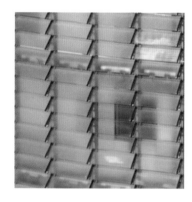

Jean Nouvel

Agbar Tower, Barcelona

Jean Nouvel

Agbar Tower, Barcelona

Jean Nouvel

Agbar Tower, Barcelona

Jean Nouvel

Agbar Tower, Barcelona

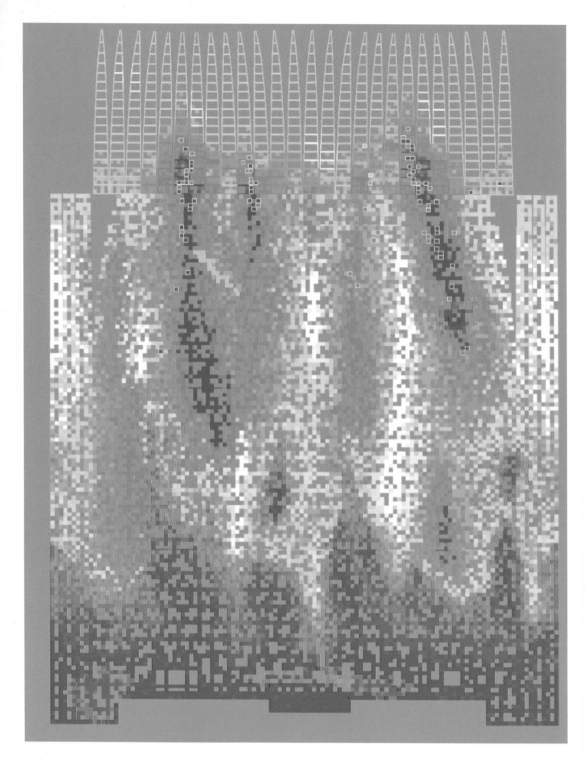

Piel Interior. Transición Cúpula-Fuste

00   07   14   35

Jean Nouvel

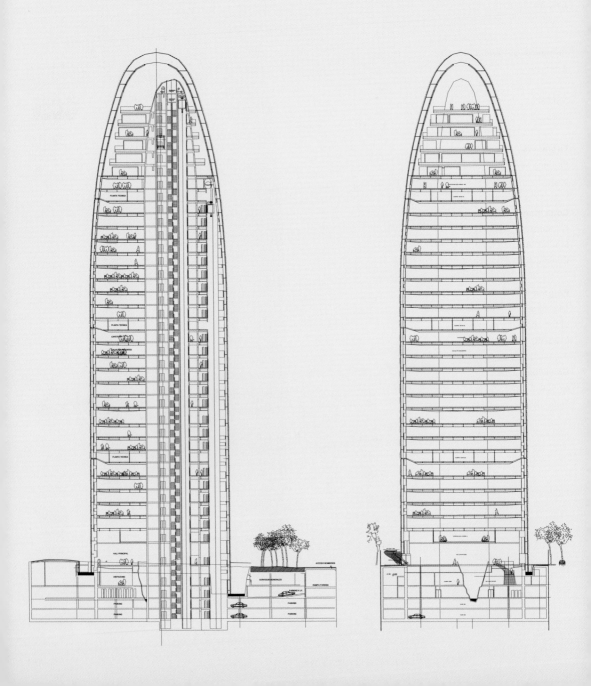

Dates
Studies: 10.1999
Construction start: 2001
Completion: 07. 2005

Client
Layetana Inmobiliaria (Barcelone – SP)

Light artist
Yann Kersalé – AIK (Paris, FR)

Graphic design
Hiroshi Maeda (Facades)

Computer-generated images
Artefactory

Model
Etienne Follenfant

Engineers
Building services: Gepro
Structure: R. Brufau & A. Obiol

Consultants
Colour study: Alain Bony
Studies: Arnauld De Bussierre
Construction: Xavier Ferres (Biosca Botey)

Programme
142-meter tower for the headquarters
of the company Aguas de Barcelona
(AGBAR) + 350-seat auditorium

Gross floor area
47.500 m² (17.500 infrastructure,
30.000 superstructure).

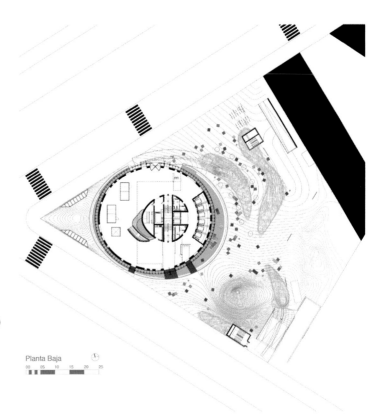

Planta Baja

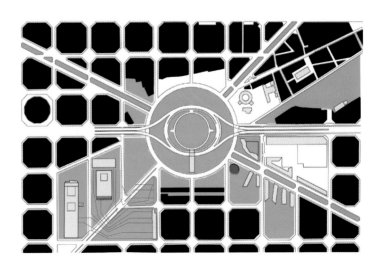

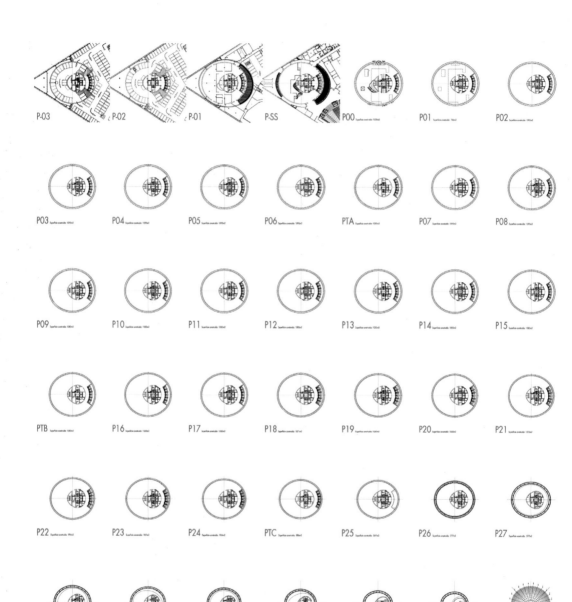

P-03 P-02 P-01 P-SS

P00 P01 P02

P03 P04 P05 P06 PTA P07 P08

P09 P10 P11 P12 P13 P14 P15

PTB P16 P17 P18 P19 P20 P21

P22 P23 P24 PTC P25 P26 P27

P28 P29 P30 P31 P31a P31b CUBIERTA

00 10 20 50

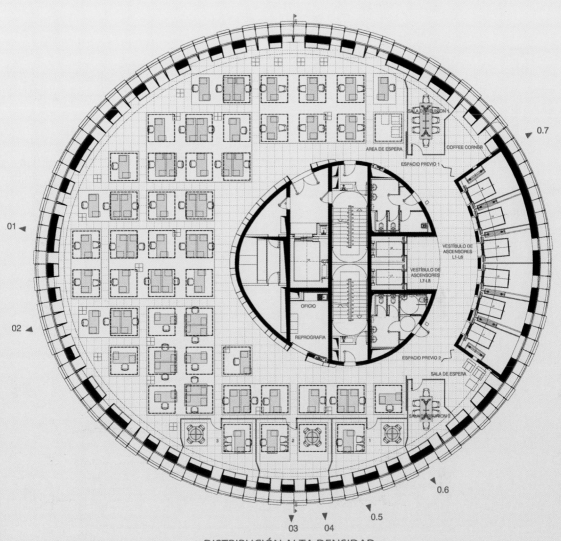

01 ◄

02 ◄

0.7 ►

0.6

0.5 ▼

03 ▼ 04 ▼

DISTRIBUCIÓN ALTA DENSIDAD

ocupación total 61 personas

DISTRIBUCIONES PLANTA TIPO.

00   02   05   10

01. Parque Güell
02. Sagrada Familia
03. Mar Mediterráneo
04. Parque de la Ciudadela
05. Barceloneta
06. Puerto Olímpico
07. Mediterráneo

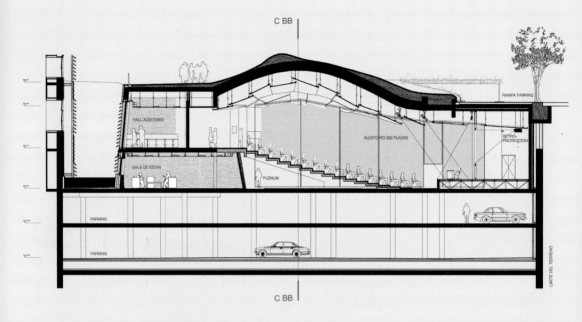

Auditorio. Sección longitudinal

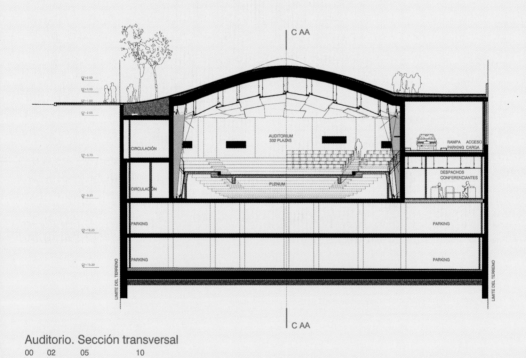

Auditorio. Sección transversal

00 02 05 10

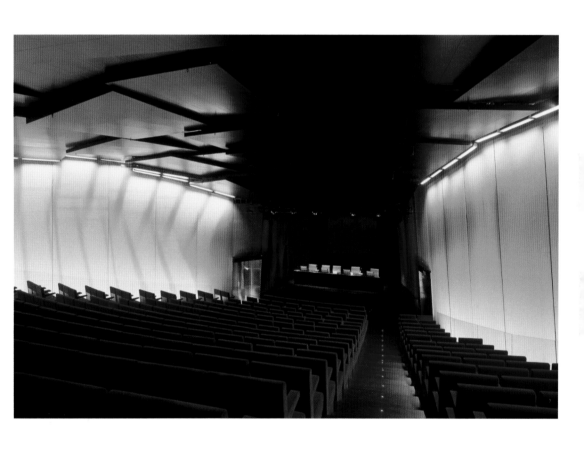

Agbar Tower, Barcelona

Jean Nouvel
Vivid red colour

'The Serpentine Pavilion 2010 in London is a contrast of lightweight materials and metal structures. The entire design is rendered in a vivid red that contrasts with the green of its park setting. The colour reflects the iconic British images of traditional telephone boxes, post boxes and London buses. The building consists of bold geometric forms, large retractable awnings and a freestanding wall that rises 12 metres above the lawn, sloping at a gravity-defying angle. Striking glass, polycarbonate and fabric structures create a versatile system of interior and exterior spaces.'

Jean Nouvel
Serpentine Pavilion, London

Jean Nouvel
Serpentine Pavilion, London

Jean Nouvel

Jean Nouvel

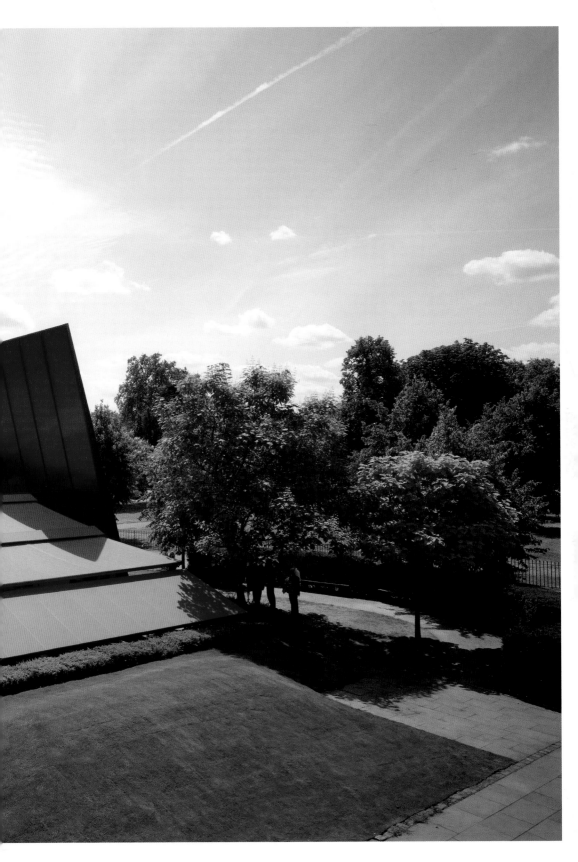

Serpentine Pavilion, London

Jean Nouvel

Serpentine Pavilion, London

Jean Nouvel
Lantern magic

'A 45-metre-high rectangular box with transparent blue "screen" walls – the Concert Hall in Copenhagen is constantly changing colour depending on the lighting conditions and time of day, both revealing and concealing the interior. At night the building lights up with images projected onto the "screen". The architecture dematerializes and becomes a matter of light and surface effects'.

Jean Nouvel

Concert Hall, Copenhagen

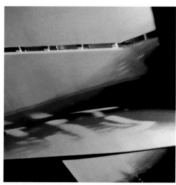

Jean Nouvel

Concert Hall, Copenhagen

Concert Hall, Copenhagen

Jean Nouvel

Jean Nouvel

Concert Hall, Copenhagen

When the Brembo Corporation decided to build its research offices and workshop facility in Bergamo alongside the Milan-Venice motorway, it was because this prestigious Italian manufacturer of brakes for luxury and competition automobiles and motorcycles wanted to be seen! Brembo is also building other commercial and hotel activities on the site. A vibrant red line, one kilometre long, runs parallel to the highway, giving this commercial-industrial ensemble a strong identity. In addition to reflecting Brembo's industrial image, the gleaming red wall of grooved, lacquered aluminium acts as a sound barrier, permitting the development of a park-like typology of buildings behind it with planted green spaces and expansive views across the landscape. The kilometre-long red screen is built over a kilometre-long parking podium that is also … red.

Jean Nouvel
A vibrant red line

 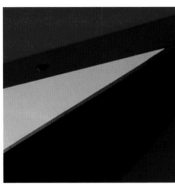

Jean Nouvel

The red kilometer, Bergamo

Jean Nouvel

The red kilometer, Bergamo

Jean Nouvel

The red kilometer, Bergamo

Jean Nouvel

The red kilometer, Bergamo

Jean Nouvel

The red kilometer, Bergamo

Wang Shu

Translating tradition for modern times

By Bert de Muynck

'For me, the most important thing is what does true experience mean? What do true materials mean, what is true construction? I'm more focused on this at the moment.'

It came to many, professionals and public alike, as a surprise when at the end of February 2012 the Chinese architect Wang Shu was announced as the recipient of the 2012 Pritzker Prize. The prize is commonly referred to as the 'Nobel Prize for Architecture' and in the past has been bestowed upon architects such as Aldo Rossi (1990), Alvaro Siza (1992), Rem Koolhaas (2000) and Eduardo Souto de Moura (2011). At the time, the recognition accorded to Wang Shu affirmed what was already common knowledge among a small group of Chinese and international architects and architecture critics: that of the few Chinese architects who have resisted the trend towards large-scale, rather bland architectural and urban environments, Wang Shu is one who over a decade of intense design activity has developed a unique way of thinking and building within the Chinese context. And that with an exceptional eye for space, materiality, gravity, detail, flow, framing, setting and structure, with an inquisitive mind that allows and seeks both the accidental and the deliberate absorption of cultural references, contextual colour and construction techniques in his architectural work.

'Without me, no design. Without her, it cannot become reality.'

The pitfalls of becoming famous

It is a sad fact that the 2012 Pritzker Prize recognises only Wang Shu, despite the fact that his office Amateur Architecture Studio is spearheaded by him and his wife, Lu Wenyu. Denying her this recognition was a regrettable mistake and shortly after the announcement Wang Shu was rather vocal in his opinion, remarking that 'Without me, no design. Without her, it cannot become reality.' [1]

[1] In a comment to the American radio-station NPR.

The worldwide recognition and acclaim that his particular Chinese architectural language (often labelled a form of 'critical regionalism') has garnered landed Wang Shu and Lu Wenyu in a seemingly never-ending storm of Chinese and international media attention, not to mention the opportunist interests of property developers and invitations to be guests of honour. Following the recognition brought by the Pritzker Prize, the Wall Street Journal proclaimed Wang Shu to be architecture's 'Innovator of the Year 2012' while TIME magazine honoured him as one the 100 Most Influential People in 2012. Lu Wenyu, however, told the Spanish newspaper *El País* in October 2013 – indirectly defending her husband for being the sole recipient of the Pritzker Prize – that 'in China, you lose your life if you become famous. I want a life and I prefer to spend it with my son. Over there I don't accept interviews. And not in English-speaking countries either [...] I'm happy to be able to do architecture that I believe helps our towns and cities to be better. I'm convinced that to talk about this awakens interest in others – not being famous.' [2]

[2] La arquitecta que renunció al Pritzker para evitar la fama, October 1, 2013, *El País* http://cultura.elpais.com/cultura/2013/09/30/actualidad/1380569553_963993.html

'In China, you lose your life if you become famous. I want a life and I prefer to spend it with my son.'

From pre- to post-Pritzker – A new angle on architecture

Smartly navigating between all the 'great opportunities' that crossed their path, Amateur Architecture Studio constructed and completed only a few projects since then – an approach that is in line with the way they see their practice. The first is the addition of a guesthouse to the existing Xiangshan Campus of the China Academy of Art in Hangzhou, the other a bus stop in the Austrian village of Krumbach. Construction on the 'Tiles Hill' project – a subtle reference to their 'Tiled Garden' installation for the 2006 Venice Architecture Biennale – in Hangzhou, a new reception centre for the Xiangshan Campus, started back in 2010, but after February 2012 construction accelerated massively, much to Wang Shu's personal and professional distaste. The size and scale of the guesthouse – featuring a 130-metre-long wooden roof, the longest of its kind in China, and rampart walls – contrasts markedly with the other recently completed project, a tiny 9-square-metre-large wooden bus stop in Austria. 'This is a bus shelter, but not merely a bus shelter,' Wang Shu remarked in an online-interview shortly after its completion. 'It is like a 120 SLR folding camera that people can sit in. It is not only an abstract lens, because the camera is built out of local wood and by local craftsmen. The lens focuses on the scenery, the symmetrical, the static; sunlight illuminates the interior as gentle breezes filter through it; our gaze is guided to the mountains far away. The symmetry of the camera will undoubtedly trigger symbolic implications, but this symmetry is broken by the sloped eaves at the side.'[3]

[3] Bus stops by Sou Fujimoto and Wang Shu shake up an Austrian village, May 16, 2014, *dezeen* http://www.dezeen.com/2014/05/16/bus-stop-project-fujimoto-shu-radic-austria/

What intrigues Wang Shu most is the way of looking, not only as an intellectual activity but also as a physical exercise for the mind and body. In an interview with Wang Shu in March 2014 conducted while he was working on the 'ADAPTATION – Architecture and Change in China' exhibition for the 2014 Venice Architecture Biennale, I discussed with him the use of the Chinese roof and the courtyard in his work, elements that I consider derive directly (albeit adapted and reinterpreted) from traditional Chinese forms and typologies. While talking about architecture and adaptation over tea, coffee and cigarettes, Wang Shu tells me: "I'm very careful when it comes to architectural references or adaptations. For example, when I design a courtyard some people will say, 'Oh this is so Chinese! It comes from China's traditions.' But usually I'm careful when designing and thinking about a courtyard. If I can't get the real feeling, a fresh feeling, I will not do it. I know about courtyards, I talk about them, but to design a courtyard isn't just a matter of designing a courtyard; one has to think seriously about it. I designed a house in Nanjing with a half-open courtyard inside, and several teaching buildings in the Xiangshan Campus in Hangzhou also feature courtyards. But this doesn't mean

'I'm very careful when it comes to architectural references or adaptations.'

By Bert de Muynck

157

these are real courtyards. My new project in the mountains of Ningbo is the first project where I have done a real courtyard. My courtyard references and inspirations come directly from different Chinese traditional paintings, most of them more than 1000 years old. These courtyards exist only in the paintings, not in reality. Painting has a different angle on and relation to reality. I like this painterly perspective because it allows you to have a different vision of reality."

Amateur versus star, original versus copy

Born in 1963, Wang Shu graduated from Nankin Institute of Technology in 1998 and undertook his doctorate at Tongji University in Shanghai in 2000. Since 2000, Wang Shu has headed the Architecture Department of the China Academy of Art in Hangzhou.

In 1997, together with Lu Wenyu, he founded Amateur Architecture Studio in Hangzhou – a 6 million-inhabitant city located about 200 kilometres southwest of Shanghai. Hangzhou is the capital of Zheijiang province and most of Amateur Architecture Studio's works are located here: the Vertical Courtyard Apartments (2002-07) and CAA Xiangshan Campus (Phase I: 2002-04; Phase II: 2004-07) in Hangzhou; the Ningbo Contemporary Art Museum (2001-05) and Ningbo History Museum (2003-08) as well as the Ceramic House (2003-06) in Jinhua.

Their office name embodies a philosophy that accommodates all forms of architecture and building principles, in contrast to the 'starchitects' who wander the world in search for opportunities to place their iconic buildings. They explain the philosophy of the office as follows: 'Built spontaneously, illegally and temporarily, amateur architecture is equal to professional architecture. But amateur architecture is just not significant. One problem of professional architecture is, that it is too concerned with the building itself.'

Since 2008 I have met and interviewed Wang Shu on many occasions and in different locations, most recently in March 2014. Sometimes we meet alone, sometimes together with Lu Wenyu. She always refuses to speak on the record and Wang Shu often refers to her as 'my secret'. They make a happy, focussed and energetic couple. They show balance and respect. He likes to smoke. Both of them have made astonishing progress in English over the past few years, putting my Chinese to shame. During a dinner in April 2012, I asked them what the Pritzker recognition means to their practice. In his typical down-to-earth manner, coupled with an often humorous, sharp, philosophical and combative state of mind, Wang Shu explains that they were 'originally just known within professional circles, but now I get public recognition. When we received the French Gold Medal from the Academy of Architecture in 2011 or the German Schelling Architecture Prize in 2010, there was no public reaction in China, even the professionals hardly paid any attention.' The reason is that Amateur Architecture Studio's architecture is far from conventional, institutional or governmental, and instead consists of sometimes hard to grasp spatial experiences that require repeated visits in order to sink in

'Built spontaneously, illegally and temporarily, amateur architecture is equal to professional architecture.'

properly. In March 2014, I asked him what has changed in these post-Pritzker times in terms of the critical reception and understanding of his work. "People – usually the younger generation – often talk about shape or movement in my architectural work," Wang Shu says. "It seems that shape or form is the easiest topic for them to discuss. In China, I have heard that there are some copies of my work in different places, some of them small, some big or even huge. People call me to ask whether I really designed a work in such-and-such a place and I tell them I have no idea and that I've never been there (laughs). 'But I found a work very similar to yours, and it so huge,' they reply. It may be influenced by my work, but then only in a very shallow way. For me it is not important whether there are copies or adaptations of my work. This is something that you can talk about, not me. All I can do is share my feelings about this."

'People – usually the younger generation – often talk about shape or movement in my architectural work.'

Time, mountains, gardens, bridges and landscape

'Amateur Architecture Studio's architecture needs time', Wang Shu told me in 2012. I remind him of our first meeting and my astonishment on seeing that the campus is still evolving and changing today: green is taking over the buildings, blending them in with their environment. He explains: 'In 2007 I talked to many people and most could not understand what would happen. The campus is more like a traditional Chinese garden: when it was just completed, it was not at its best. You have to wait, maybe even ten years, for it to grow. My architecture needs time to change. In the beginning it is like a small chicken without feathers. Or like wine, or tea… it needs time.'

I tell him that time – in the rapidly changing urban and economic context of contemporary China – is a luxury. The architectural and urban stakes and the ambitions in this country are high, the speed of construction fast. In 2009, the McKinsey Global Institute predicted that if current trends continue, China's urban population will expand from 572 million in 2005 to 926 million in 2025 and hit the one billion mark by 2030. In 20 years, China's cities will have expanded to accommodate a further 350 million people. That is as if the entire Dutch population were to move to the cities every year. The result of this rush, coupled with a demand for property among the rising middle-class, is an urban environment that is at best bland and certainly problematic: massive repetitive housing blocks, a confused preference for neo-classical architecture, shrinking farmland, disappearing rural villages, displaced communities and oversized shopping malls and pseudo-futuristic office towers in the cities' growing central business districts. And in-between all of that, an impressive new network of roads, railways, subways and airports has been, or is in the process of being constructed.

'My architecture needs time to change. In the beginning it is like a small chicken without feathers. Or like wine, or tea… it needs time.'

Amateur Architecture Studio's philosophy of design in and with time is exemplified in what is arguably the office's most architectural tour-de-force to date: the Hangzhou Xiangshan Campus of the China Academy of Art (CAA). Founded in 1928 in Hangzhou, the China Academy of Art is the most reputable university of art in China. While the administrative headquarters of the Academy are located on the Nanshan Campus, on the banks of the beautiful West Lake in Hangzhou, the Xiangshan Central Campus is an extension of the CAA located about 15 kilometres to the southwest, behind a range of mountains. The campus is spread out on the site like a necklace around the picturesque Xiangshan (Elephant) Mountain. Around this mountain Amateur Architecture Studio have built, in two phases, probably the most intriguing piece of architecture in China in the last decade.

The campus covers an area of 530,000 square metres, nearly half of which is occupied by hills and pools of water. The buildings of the first phase all rise from a similar stone platform, reminiscent of the architecture local farmers use to grow tea in the mountains. The second phase took fourteen months to build and was finished in early 2008.

In 2008 when I visited the campus, Wang Shu took me on a three-hour walk through phase I and II, explaining along the way that they designed it with the idea of creating a new type of city: 'We have lost the tradition of how to build cities, how to build architecture that relates to its landscape. The campus is a new model for our Chinese cities, featuring high-density areas where buildings are very close to each other. The distance between them is the shortest possible, according to the Chinese laws.' The different buildings are connected by bridges, lifting the architecture, its studios, classrooms and libraries, above the landscape, creating a constant dialogue between the openness of the landscape and the closeness of the buildings. These bridges transform seamlessly into corridors that are wide enough to serve as places to teach, or else widen into platforms, seamlessly connecting different teaching rooms and courtyards with each other.

'We have lost the tradition of how to build cities, how to build architecture that relates to its landscape.'

The strategy of on-site teaching

Over the years, I have learned more about his way of working, not only in his studio, but also on site. In our last interview he explained how he deals with the constraints of time, experience, budget and ambition in China: 'Usually at the beginning, the client, engineer and construction workers worry about the technical solutions and ask themselves and me if they can really do this. "We don't have any experience of how to do this," they say and ask me what I want them to do. I just talk to them and tell them that they are capable, that they have the experience but don't realize it. Only gradually, by working, do they understand that they really can do it. At the same time, they still need direction on site, a bit of teaching, which results in making changes, sometimes many times. I keep everything precise, and sometimes what they do is not good enough, or even very bad. But for me, everything is good as long as they maintain a level of precision. Maybe other architects would have it demolished and rebuilt if they didn't like it. I don't do that. That's life. I just follow the process. It is also a very practical thing. If they have to demolish something, it affects the budget, as time is lost. This is about life, my way of doing things, and I enjoy it.'

'This is about life, my way of doing things, and I enjoy it.'

Typhoons, tiles and traditions

For the 2006 Architecture Biennial in Venice, Amateur Architecture Studio designed a tiled garden, an installation made of 66,000 recycled tiles, salvaged from demolition sites.

Almost every building on the campus features similar tiles used either for roofing, in walls, as floor materials, as part of the landscape. 'All the tiles are recycled,' Wang Shu told me in 2008. 'I want to promote debate on the re-use of materials. They come from the Zhejiang province, where many old towns and houses were demolished, and they are considered rubbish. Sustainable architecture is not about using expensive high-tech materials, but about doing simple things. The overall feeling is that the tiles are a connection with tradition.'

'This old and beautiful material is very cheap.'

Another facade is built out of a somewhat random pattern of bricks of all shapes, colours and sizes. "In the East part of this province, near the sea, there are many typhoons, which routinely cause houses to collapse. Because the residents do not have a lot of time to rebuild them, they put the bricks back together randomly. I find this a very beautiful method."

But besides this notion of recycling and re-using traditional materials, there is also an economic aspect. Wang Shu explains: 'This old and beautiful material is very cheap. This is how I convince my client. Usually my budgets are very low, so it is of interest to them. In China, we face a strange situation: when you build with machinery, it is very expensive, but when you build by hand it becomes cheaper.'

Childhood memories: hutong walls and sheep horns

Wang Shu was born in 1963 in Urumqi, a city in Xinjiang, the western-most province of the People's Republic of China. His father is a musician as well as an amateur carpenter, his mother a teacher of young children and a school librarian. As a young child he would often have to travel 4,000 kilometres between Urumqi and Beijing, a journey that took four days and four nights by train. These travels afforded him the opportunity to experiencing the vast, changing landscapes as he grew up.

When we spoke in 2012, he talked fondly about his memories of going to Beijing and living in the old quarters of the city: 'I lived in a hutong (alley-way) in Beijing for almost 3 years during which I drew many things on the hutong walls. In 1969 I left Beijing, only to return 3 years later. My drawings were still there. I was surprised. Many old people told me that they guard-ed my painting, preventing the wall from being knocked down because it held Wang Shu's paintings. It is still there, in the Jianguomen area, near a very small group of about ten courtyards, with big buildings around it.'

Lu Wenyu was also born in Xinjiang province. I ask them if they consider Hangzhou their home. He responds with a quick and affirmative 'No' fol-lowed by: 'My birthplace is in Xinjiang. But now I think, maybe Hangzhou should become my hometown. Both of us feel like people who have made a long trip, crossing the desert and ocean in order to settle down. Originally, we did not like it here that much and my wife wanted to go back. I also love Xinjiang, as it has an unbelievable landscape. Did you know that I used the ride the sheep, the very big ones? It is easy: you take it by the horns and ride it.' We all laugh while he repeats the story, this time in Chinese, to his son who looks surprised.

Searching for the true meaning of architecture

Winning the Pritzker Prize might have come as a surprise to many as until

recently he was fairly unknown and not even particularly acclaimed in

China. That is changing, he says, in 2012, with a hint of irony: 'In the past

many people criticised the design of the China Academy of Art campus

and now many people say they love it. That is a big change.' At the time

I ask how this recognition affected their work. 'After the announcement

of the Pritzker Prize I hardly had time to work. There were too many

interviews – for television, newspapers or magazines – all competing for

my attention. So the only thing I could do at that time was to finish my

old work. I couldn't accept any new commissions, because I have a small

studio and teach at the school as well.'

Amateur Architecture Studio's particular way of working provokes not

only the creation of exceptional architectural work, but is also very time

and energy consuming. Upon being announced the winner of Pritzker

Prize, Wang Shu's immediate public reaction, during a lecture in Los An-

'My dream is to stop working, to have a one-year rest and continue again after that.'

geles, was that it came rather unexpected: 'I wanted to take two years off

work, because my son is ten. But then I won the Pritzker Prize, and now I

don't think I can stop.' The need to take a break was already something

he had mentioned to me often, even before receiving public recognition:

'I have many different projects going on now and that is a good feeling

but also very tiring. My dream is to stop working, to have a one-year rest

and continue again after that.' But this rest does not look like it will hap-

pen soon. In 2012 I reminded him about this, asking how the recognition he had received had changed his ideas about taking a break. 'A lot of people ask me if my life will change,' he says, 'but if there's one thing I am clear about, it is that there is no reason to change, no need for that. I will still maintain my way of life, which means that my way is that I do not want to change.'

Having had hardly any break from China's demanding architectural culture, I asked him again in March 2014 if he still planned to realise his long-held plan to take a rest. While admitting it is a difficult yet necessary thing to do, Wang Shu gently steered his answer in a different direction, revealing a glimpse of the responsibility he now feels as a contemporary Chinese architect: 'For me, the most important thing is what does true experience mean? What do true materials mean, what is true construction? I'm more focused on this at the moment. In modern society in China today, almost everything is fake, everything is copied and you rarely find anything that's true. I want to talk about this, the true meaning of this situation.'

Wang Shu is one of the few Chinese architects with a clear insight into the mechanisms underlying the development – or 'non-development' – of architecture and cities in China. 'In China we have lost the tradition of building cities and of creating architecture that is part of the landscape. In my design for the Hangzhou campus, for instance, I positioned the buildings at the foot of the Xiangshan (Elephant) Mountain in such a way that each building enters into a different dialogue with the mountain, offering various views of it.

Wang Shu
Old and beautiful material

To me, a building as an object isn't important.

It's the building's relation to nature that interests me most.'

Wang Shu's architecture is neither a protest nor an alternative to the soulless work, both foreign and domestic, that is preventing China from building a future distinctly its own. In search of identity and creativity, Wang Shu explores the rich legacy of China's intellectual and architectural history and subsequently takes a seemingly simple approach to architecture that culminates in astonishing creations. Wang Shu in conversation with Bert de Muynck / MovingCities

Wang Shu

Historic Museum, Ningbo

Wang Shu

Historic Museum, Ningbo

Wang Shu

Historic Museum, Ningbo

Wang Shu

Historic Museum, Ningbo

Historic Museum, Ningbo

Wang Shu
Traditional Chinese garden

The buildings are arranged around the southern side of the mountain, in a manner typical of Wang Shu's approach.

The plan creates complex and unexpected relationships between the buildings and the landscape. Exposed corners jar with formal elevations and informal vistas are framed by semi-enclosed courtyards or jagged openings in concrete walls that recall the patterned windows of traditional Chinese gardens. The entire scheme is crisscrossed by elevated walkways that wind their diagonal course around and through the buildings breaking down the horizontality of the facades and binding together the whole scheme.

Wang Shu

Park Pavilion, Jinhua

Wang Shu
Park Pavilion, Jinhua

Wang Shu

Park Pavilion, Jinhua

'An important aspect of the design is the "free" concept. This "free" concept is not just about its architectural form, but its sensitive response to the site and nature.'
Wang Shu, Lu Wenyu.

Wang Shu
Architecture needs time to change

The Chinese character for 'enclose' was the theme of the buildings, and courtyards and gardens are therefore a very important aspect. These enclosed spaces serve many purposes in each building – as a place for events, gatherings, classes and relaxation as well as for climate control to help encourage ventilation and to create a microclimate. The choice of themes follows traditional cultural patterns of construction and their continuation: garden making, construction, differentiation, material recycling and re-use.

Wang Shu

China Academy of Art, Hangzhou

China Academy of Art, Hangzhou

Wang Shu

China Academy of Art, Hangzhou

Wang Shu

China Academy of Art, Hangzhou

Wang Shu

China Academy of Art, Hangzhou

Wang Shu and Lu Wenyu
Meditation and poetry

The architecture of the guesthouse and reception centre Wa Shan addresses roles that are dear to the Amateur Architecture Studio run by Wang Shu and Lu Wenyu: how vernacular traditions can be embedded in contemporary forms, how architecture can relate to and transform the natural environment in which it is placed in many intricate ways, and how materials, spaces and visual elements can convey an atmosphere of meditation and poetry...

Wang Shu and *Lu Wenyu*
Wa Shan Guesthouse, Hangzhou

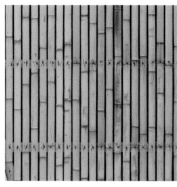

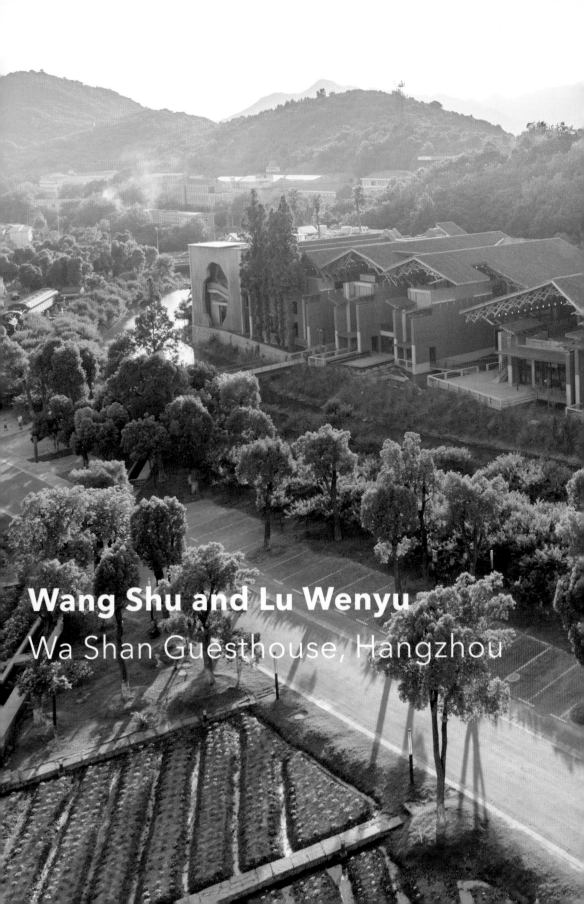

Wang Shu and Lu Wenyu
Wa Shan Guesthouse, Hangzhou

Wang Shu and Lu Wenyu

Wa Shan Guesthouse, Hangzhou

Wang Shu and Lu Wenyu

Wa Shan Guesthouse, Hangzhou

Wang Shu and Lu Wenyu

Wa Shan Guesthouse, Hangzhou

Wang Shu and Lu Wenyu

Wa Shan Guesthouse, Hangzhou

Wang Shu and Lu Wenyu

Wa Shan Guesthouse, Hangzhou

Colour in perspective
Vision and perception

By Erik Mattie

'We have established the true place of colour in architecture and so declare that painting without architectural construction (that is, easel-painting) has no further reason for existence' [1]

[1] Theo van Doesburg, Cornelis van Eesteren. Towards a collective construction. De Stijl, VI, 6/7, 1924, pp 89-91.

> 'Good architects
> have a vision of colour
> and the surroundings,
> a talent that is held
> in high regard by
> discerning clients.'

Much has been written about colour and architecture, not least by architects themselves. Through the nature of their profession, architects have a strong visual focus and generally have well-developed perceptive skills. Good architects have a vision of colour and the surroundings, a talent that is held in high regard by discerning clients. The built environment should ideally reflect the most perfect colour swatch conceivable. Unfortunately, reality rarely conforms to ideals and is more complex and less mouldable than clients and members of municipal aesthetics committees would wish. There are many reasons, first and foremost time, although too often, architects and clients alike choose to regard time as a negligible quantity: here we mean time in the sense of the past - the historically layered context - and time in the sense of the future. The effect of a colour is always relative to the ever-changing colour palette of its immediate surroundings.

Architects who build within a historic context - anxious to avoid thoughtless copying - often look to blend in with what is already there: taking the genius loci or more prosaically the vernacular, the local building tradition,

as inspiration. Introduced by Christian Norberg-Schulz in 1980 in his

influential book Genius Loci: Towards a Phenomenology of Architecture,

the idea of the 'genius' or atmosphere of a place was not exclusively

defined by the material or form. Aspects such as light (climate) and

colour also contribute to its unique personality of place. But achieving

a full understanding of this unique personality would be a near super-

human feat, requiring that the architect possess not only a utopian capacity

for relating to the specific area but also unlimited knowledge of the area

at his disposal. What constitutes the local characteristic may manifest

itself in many forms over the course of generations, and colour, too, is

subject to the whims of fashion. Nevertheless, the result, the sum of various

subsequent architectural styles and movements within a historically

layered context, is what constitutes a single unique locus.

Due to its complexity, achieving a full understanding of the 'spirit of a

place' requires research. Research into historical colours is a relatively

'Aspects such as light (climate) and colour also contribute to its unique personality of place.'

young, separate discipline within the field of building history and has revealed some surprising findings over the past decades. A constant factor in local colour is the colour of the predominant building material. In London, light yellow sandstone was widely won and used, whereas Dutch cities are mostly built of red brick. The brightly coloured, glazed roof tiles of Burgundy can also be considered part of the vernacular. In addition to material colour, the paint hues and pigments are also components of local tradition. But despite tradition, this local colour palette is much less constant than is generally assumed. Until as late as the 1980s the general consensus was that the paint used for the woodwork of patrician houses in Amsterdam was limited to two historical colours: so-called canal green and off-white. Recent research has shown that these colours were actually predominantly used in the 19th century and were preceded by other, more original colours, that later became obsolete. This is also true of other Dutch cities. Research in Dordrecht and Leiden revealed a bright colour palette that was previously considered inconceivable.

These results make it evident that a sense of colour or taste is at least in part dependent on the perception of colour within a specific, historical context. The same is true for the perception of white, the *absence* of colour. The pristine white marble statues and buildings from classical times are etched in the visual memory of the observer, much like the iconic buildings of 1920s modernism. The dogma of white marble antiquity was disproven as early as the 19th century, by an architect no less: Jacques-Ignace Hittorff (1792–1867). The other dogma, of ethereal white facades, upheld by many until relatively recently, has never really disappeared.

The concept of white, modern and therefore progressive architecture is in part based on completed projects with ominous names such as the *Weiße Stadt* in Berlin and the *Weißenhofsiedlung* near Stuttgart. White is neutral and a neutral colour scheme befits puritanical, deliberately ornament-free modernists. But the concept is also based on the many black and white photographs from that era, and that concept is distorted. *Onkel Toms Hütte* by Bruno Taut, a housing estate in the leafy area of Berlin features an extremely well thought out colour scheme of facades painted with keim and brightly coloured woodwork (keim is a mineral paint that attaches easily to stone, patented in 1878). The individual low-rise houses are designed based on standard elements, with a number of different variations within that standard. A striking variable is colour: two colours of keim for every facade, from a palette of a total of eight colours and the woodwork in a matching scheme of even more different colours (twelve types). White is the exception, colour the rule. The interiors of these modernist interbellum buildings were also colourful, not bright white. White interior walls only became popular in the sixties. As a result of this new fashion, the walls of the earlier generations were also stripped of their wallpaper and painted white, much like the removal of the polychrome plasterwork in Catholic churches throughout Europe to reveal the honest brickwork beneath. A well-known example is the Sonneveld house in Rotterdam (Brinkman & Van der Vlugt, 1933), the renowned director's villa. Research conducted prior to its restoration revealed that the house was much more colourful than old pictures seemed to suggest. Other examples also abound: the Rietveld-Schroeder house

White is neutral and a neutral colour scheme befits puritanical, deliberately ornament-free modernists.

By Erik Mattie

229

in Utrecht, the Parisian *Maison de Verre* by Pierre Charreau and Bijvoet or the green onyx in the Barcelona pavilion by Mies van der Rohe all prove that colour and interior, as well as colour and architecture are inseparable pairs. Modernist colours were no less bright than those of the Jugendstil; they were simply different.

The fact that the colours of the past and therefore those of the present are open to multiple interpretations is therefore evident, but time is also a defining factor in the colour schemes of the future. Modern paint is more UV resistant than ever before, but even exterior walls painted with synthetic paints require maintenance. Often, the colour used for maintenance differs ever so slightly from the original, until the original is lost forever. Colours weather or gain a patina that is valued, such as the green hue of oxidised copper. Fashion again may play a decisive role in the choice of a totally different colour combination, and the colours of the surroundings are also subject to change.

The combination of decline (and maintenance) and history will lead to a certain perception of the colour palette and its subsequent modification, a process that repeats itself with every new generation. Colours are not around forever, just for a decade or two. Which leaves the architect with the underappreciated task of looking at the surroundings from a fresh perspective to decide whether his choice of colour responds to the surroundings, whether it blends in or poses a contrast. In extraordinary cases, an architect may choose a colour that deviates completely from

'All prove that colour and interior, as well as colour and architecture are inseparable pairs.'

Colour in perspective

the context and even detracts from the architecture itself. After much deliberation, architect Jean-Michel Wilmotte, responsible for the interior of the new Rijksmuseum in Amsterdam, chose four shades of grey as the perfect backdrop for displaying works of art. The original, 19th century architecture made of brick with natural stone cross ribs, designed by P.J.H. Cuypers and influenced by the renowned French architect and theoretician Eugène Viollet-le-Duc, is much more defined by the material and colour contrasts than it is by a uniform layer of wall paint. In this case, the essence of the building was deemed subordinate to its function as a museum. However, Sikkens did develop a special colour fan deck – based on Cuypers' colours – for those components of the building that were treated from a restorative perspective, including the spectacular 19th century library.

Time and the perception of colour are therefore closely related. How-ever, there is another factor that has a huge impact on the perception of colours, which is the weather – where the unit for calculation is not a generation, but an hour or even less. The effect on the built environment can hardly be overrated. Light and shadow can promote mediocre archi-tecture to art, and conversely, a brightly painted facade on a sunny day may leave the observer gasping for air. The perception of colour can vary from minute to minute on any given day. This is true for the perception of industrial, synthetic paints, but also for the perception of material colours. Clients from Copenhagen, Hamburg and Birmingham paying a visit to Bar-celona or Milan would be wise to leave their coloured sunglasses at home.

'Time and the perception of colour are therefore closely related.'

By Erik Mattie

To conclude, we may state that the perception of colour is both subjective and time-defined. Furthermore, the range of available colours has become limitless over the past years. A computer can now mix any desired colour. In 1928, Taut had 56 colour tones to choose from. When the estate was renovated in 1978, the range had grown to 250, including the historic colours. When Aldo Rossi built his multi-coloured building block on Berlin's Charlottenstrasse he was able to choose from no less than ten thousand colours. Every year sees the addition of thousands of new colours to the colour swatches. But more colours are not necessarily an asset. While an architect can now employ a colour palette of his own creation, he has no influence on the surroundings, much less the weather. These totally and partially unpredictable factors, in combination with a completely overwhelming range of colours, make the choice infinitely more complex. Thankfully, as stated at the outset, good architects have a vision of colour and the surroundings. And generally speaking, they know what they're doing.

'But more colours are not necessarily an asset.'

Reference literature

Norberg-Schulz, Christian, *Genius Loci: Towards a Phenomenology of Architecture*. Academy Editions Ltd, London 1980.

Pitz, Helge; Brenne, Winfried, *Die Bauwerke und Kunstdenkmäler von Berlin, Beiheft 1, Bezirk Zehlendorf.*

Siedlung Onkel Tom. Einfamilienreihenhäuser 1929. Architekt Bruno Taut. Gebr. Mann Verlag, Berlin 1980.

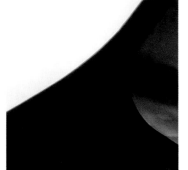

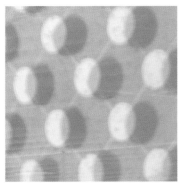

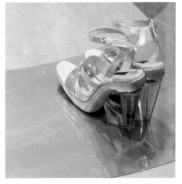

At the centre of the pool is the statue that has become a symbol for Denmark: 'The Little Mermaid'. The pavilion is a monolithic structure in white painted steel which keeps it cool during the hot Shanghai summers. The roof has a light blue surface texture, the same as that used for Danish cycle paths. Inside, the floor has a white epoxy coating except for the blue cycle path that passes through the building. The steel facade is perforated in a pattern that reflects the building's structure.

'Gradually we all get the feeling that sustainable life simply is less fun than normal life. If sustainable designs are to become competitive it can not be for purely moral or political reasons, they have to be more attractive and desirable than the non-sustainable alternative. With the Danish Pavilion we have attempted to consolidate a handful of real experiences of how a sustainable city, such as Copenhagen, can in fact increase the quality of life.' *Bjarke Ingels* of *BIG*

BIG

Danish Pavilion, EXPO 2010,

Shanghai

BIG
Light blue texture

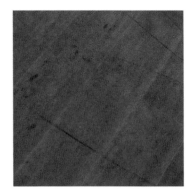 

Danish Pavilion, EXPO 2010, Shanghai

BIG

Danish Pavilion, EXPO 2010, Shanghai

BIG

Danish Pavilion, EXPO 2010, Shanghai

Danish Pavilion, EXPO 2010, Shanghai

Superkilen is one of the most ethnically diverse neighbourhoods in Copenhagen. The Superkilen project by Danish architects BIG, in collaboration with German landscape architects Topotek1 and the Copenhagen-based art group Superflex, is subtitled 'Public Participation Extreme'.

The master plan for the park, stretching approximately one kilometre from Nørrebrogade to Tagensvej, has been divided into three areas, each with a different colour to mark specific functions.

The Red Square is directly connected to Nørrebro's busiest street, the Nørrebrogade, and functions as Superkilen's link to the city. It is also an extension of the existing sports centre, Nørrebrohallen, and offers additional areas for outdoor urban sports and fitness. This, coupled with the Jamaican sound system, gives the area a distinctly youthful vibe.

The Black Square plays a central part in the master plan. Devised as an urban living room, it offers areas for more contemplative, introverted activities and is a setting for social gatherings and flea markets on the weekends.

The Green Park with its soft, grassy hills is family-friendly and an obvious picnic spot.

BIG
Colour coded master plan

BIG

Superkilen Urban Park, Copenhagen

SuperKilen Urban Park, Copenhagen

BIG
SuperKilen Urban Park, Copenhagen

SuperKilen Urban Park, Copenhagen

The complex of buildings includes a conference centre, exhibition venue, hotel and marina, and a quay for 700 boats in Sardinia. On the site of a former military arsenal on the island of La Maddalena, the mixed-use complex is a combination of new buildings and conversions, all designed and built to respect the natural landscape and follow principles of sustainable architecture. The Conference Hall, the most representative of the interventions, is a glass and basalt prism that cantilevers over the water. La Maddalena is a model of sustainable practices designed to improve and preserve the extraordinary qualities of the Mediterranean landscape and the natural biodiversity of the archipelago.

It conserves resources, using seawater for heating and cooling the buildings, and takes advantage of renewable resources, such as wind and sun.

Stefano Boeri
Glass and basalt prism

Stefano Boeri

Complex of Buildings at

La Maddalena, Sardinia

Stefano Boeri

Complex of Buildings at La Maddalena, Sardinia

Stefano Boeri

Complex of Buildings at La Maddalena, Sardinia

Stefano Boeri

Complex of Buildings at La Maddalena, Sardinia

'Not an object-container, but rather a campus for art', where flows and pathways overlap and connect, in order to create a dynamic and interactive space.
'A new fluid kind of spatiality of multiple perspective points and fragmented geometry, designed to embody the chaotic fluidity of modern life'. *Zaha Hadid.*

Zaha Hadid
Suspended black

Natural lighting has been achieved through the use of thin concrete beams on the ceiling, together with glass covering and filtering systems. The same beams have a bottom rail from which artwork can be suspended.

The beams, staircases and linear lighting system guide visitors through the interior walkway, which ends in a large space on the third level. From here, a large window offers a view over the city.

Zaha Hadid

MAXXI Museum, Rome

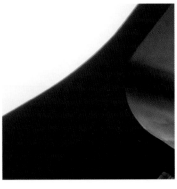

Zaha Hadid

MAXXI Museum, Rome

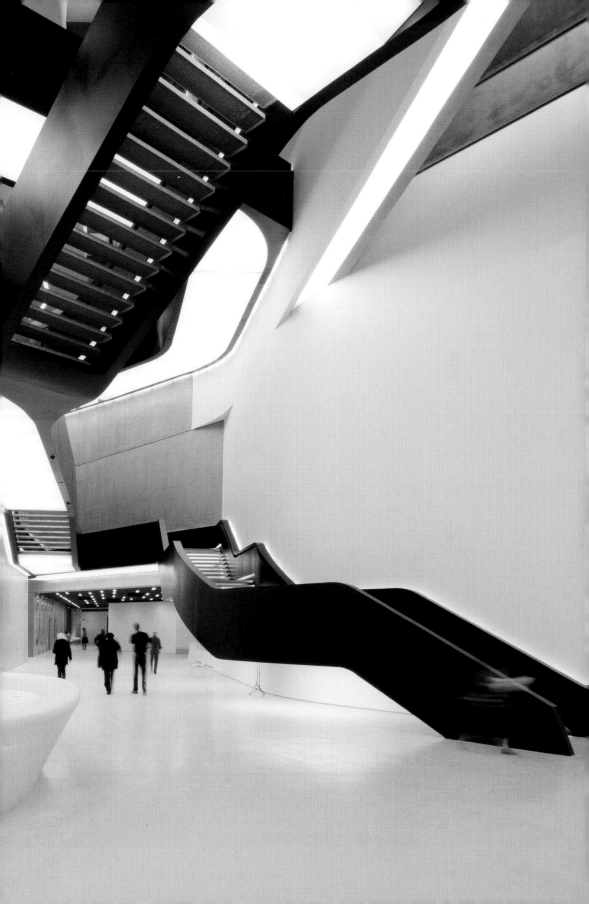

Zaha Hadid

MAXXI Museum, Rome

Zaha Hadid

MAXXI Museum, Rome

28 condominiums within a strictly defined criterion. The porch is separated from the street by a cast aluminium gate, a physical barrier as well as a visual screen. The gate is a collage of graffiti tags, translated into three dimensions.

Herzog & de Meuron
Many shades of green

 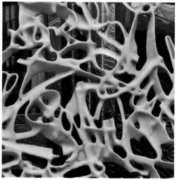

The structure of the building is pushed to the exterior and follows the grid of the large floor-to-ceiling window bays. The slabs and columns are clad with gently curved glass covers, which wrap over the structure and can be read as a continuation of the windowpanes. On the one hand the skeleton and bones of the building are expressed, on the other they melt into the glass surface of the window bays and dissolve in a play of translucency, light and reflection.

The colour of the building is the colour of the glass, with its many shades of green, which depend on the light, viewing angle, thickness and the glass layering.

Herzog & de Meuron

28 Condominiums at

40 Bond Street, New York

Herzog & de Meuron

28 Condominiums at
40 Bond Street, New York

28 Condominiums at 40 Bond Street, New York

Herzog & de Meuron

Herzog & de Meuron

28 Condominiums at 40 Bond Street, New York

The Linked Hybrid apartment complex, sited adjacent to the site of the old city wall of Beijing, aims to counter current urban developments in China by creating a new 21st century permeable urban space, inviting and open to the public from every side. The ground level offers a number of open passages for all people, residents and visitors alike, to walk through. Shops activate the urban space surrounding the large reflecting pond. On the intermediate level of the lower buildings, public roof gardens offer tranquil green spaces, and at the top of the eight residential towers private roof gardens are connected to the penthouses. All public functions on the ground level, including a restaurant, hotel, Montessori school, kindergarten and cinema are connected to the green spaces surrounding the project. From the 12th to the 18th floor, a multi-functional series of sky bridges with a swimming pool, fitness room, café, gallery, auditorium and a mini salon connects the eight residential towers and the hotel tower, offering spectacular views.

Steven Holl Architects
Open colour

Steven Holl Architects

Linked Hybrid

Apartment Complex, Beijing

Steven Holl Architects

Linked Hybrid

Apartment Complex, Beijing

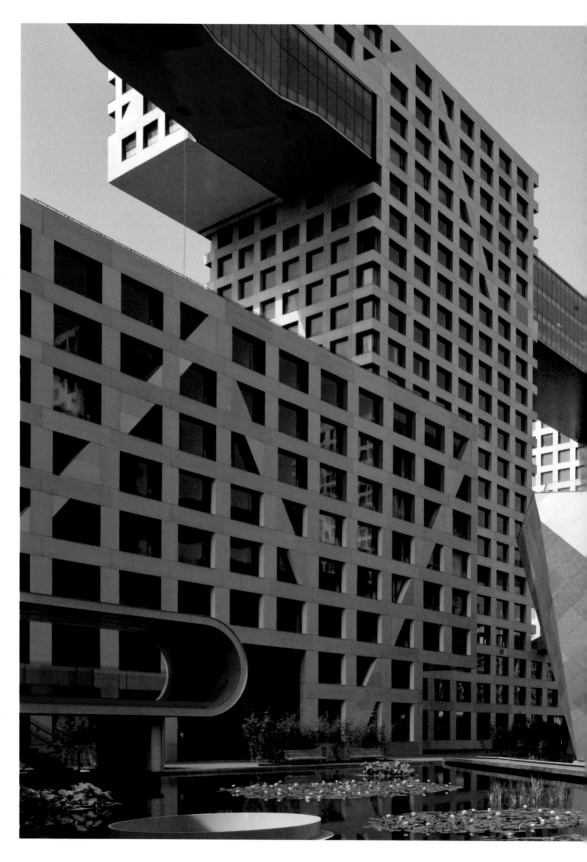

Steven Holl Architects

Linked Hybrid Apartment Complex, Beijing

Steven Holl Architects

Linked Hybrid Apartment Complex, Beijing

Steven Holl Architects

Linked Hybrid Apartment Complex, Beijing

'As regards the sense and meaning
of technology, this is something I
now hide so you can't see it. It is an
element to be used and exploited
in an indirect way. My concern
is with architecture that you can
touch and feel, the physical reality
of the object. This is what interests
me.' *Toyo Ito* in conversation with
Stefano Mirti.

Toyo Ito
Polished painted colour

The tower is basically a rectangular
box, and from a distance resembles a typical skyscraper. However,
it is at its most appealing at night,
when different coloured lights
make the irregular windows glow,
revealing the glamorous interior.

Toyo Ito

Mikimoto Ginza 2, Tokyo

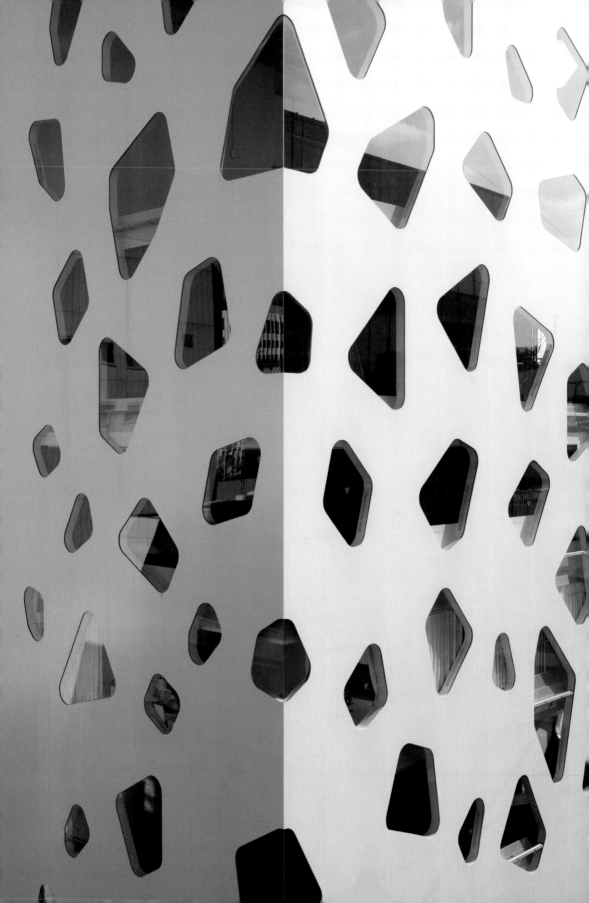

Toyo Ito
Mikimoto Ginza 2,
Tokyo

Mikimoto Ginza 2, Tokyo

Toyo Ito

The form is inspired by the makeshift tents that are commonly erected after an earthquake. The exterior is plastered in a dark grey similar to that of the makeshift tents, while the interior is painted pink in memory of the girl's favourite colour.

Lui Jiakun
Favourite colour pink

Some articles chronicling her short life are hung on the walls. A round skylight fills the space with light, making this tiny space pure and delicately charming. The memorial is, after all, erected in memory of a simple, young girl who was the light of her parents' lives.

Liu Jiakun learned about Hu three days after her death while volunteering his services at the Juyuan Middle School, where parents claim shoddy construction was mainly to blame for the death of about 900 students.

Liu Jiakun: 'I am a father of an eight year old. I can hardly imagine what it would be like to see my son under that rubble. I really wanted to do something for the family.'

Lui Jiakun

Hu Huishan Earthquake Memorial, Sichuan

Lui Jiakun

Hu Huishan Earthquake Memorial, Sichuan

Lui Jiakun

Hu Huishan Earthquake Memorial, Sichuan

Lui Jiakun

Hu Huishan Earthquake Memorial, Sichuan

The Carver Apartments provide permanent housing for formerly homeless elderly and disabled residents, and is a place for solace, support and individual growth in the face of the city's chronic homeless problem. By incorporating communal spaces, kitchens, dining areas, gathering spaces and gardens into the Carver's raised form, as well as medical and social support facilities into the plinth beneath, the project encourages its residents to reconnect with each other and the city beyond. At the street level, a series of lines trace across the building's plinth, these primary circulation paths create views deep into and across the block. Individual studio apartments are arrayed off this central courtyard area on the five floors above. A series of fins trace across the circular edge of the central space as it rises through the building, creating a rhythm of light and shadow across the gathering spaces below.

Michael Malzan Architecture
Rhythm of light and shadow

Michael Malzan Architecture

New Carver Apartments,

Los Angeles

Michael Malzan Architecture
New Carver Apartments, Los Angeles

Michael Malzan Architecture

New Carver Apartments, Los Angeles

Michael Malzan Architecture

The Inner City Arts campus provides arts education for at-risk young people from Los Angeles state schools each year. The campus houses a range of art facilities and is an oasis in the urban environment. Children create: ceramics, dance, painting, sculpture or animation.

An aggregate of diverse, interwoven forms, the campus design highlights the interplay of physical and programmatic elements. Within, the space of the courtyard and the studios weave a texture of form, light and colour. The ceramics tower beckons as a symbol of the connections forged between students, the community and the world at large.

Michael Malzan Architecture
Texture, form, light and colour

Michael Malzan Architecture

Inner City Arts Campus,

Los Angeles

Inner City Arts Campus, Los Angeles

Michael Malzan Architecture

Inner City Arts Campus, Los Angeles

Michael Malzan Architecture

Inner City Arts Campus, Los Angeles

The school is a centre for children, teachers and family. Its design is a response to the pragmatic need to enable more children to attend the school in Santa Marta in the future. The modular concept allows new groupings to be linked in various configurations and extended as far as the site permits. Following the morphology of the site, a system has been devised based on a typical module that fulfils the requirements of the architectural programme as well as the spatial needs of the education centre. It creates meeting places and play areas so that the school can function as a learning mechanism. The module is designed as a flexible and neutral space that can accommodate multiple activities and facilitates a close relationship between the children and teachers.

Giancarlo Mazzanti
Interrelated colour

 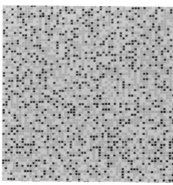

Giancarlo Mazzanti
Timayui School, Santa Marta

Giancarlo Mazzanti

Timayui School,
Santa Marta

Giancarlo Mazzanti

Timayui School, Santa Marta

Giancarlo Mazzanti

Timayui School, Santa Marta

A completely green 32-metre-high building with randomly placed transparent bubbles, the Media-Tic was conceived to establish links between state agencies and technology-media communications firms. It serves as an international platform for economic innovation and information and is an example of digital architecture. The fully visible metal frame is suspended rather than pre-stressed, and is coated with an aero-chemical paint that makes it appear bio-luminous at night. Each facade is different and reflects the research that has gone into sustainability and materials. The interior has a spacious lobby and the floors are not anchored to the exterior walls and are therefore flexible. This is made possible by concentrating the services and vertical communication ducts at the extremities.

The oppressive feeling created by the low ceiling heights is offset by the panoramic views from within. The planted roof also offers fine views of the city.

Enric Ruiz-Geli, Cloud 9
Transparant colour

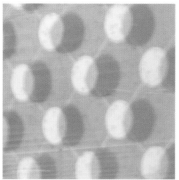

Enric Ruiz-Geli, Cloud 9

Media Tic Building, Barcelona

Enric Ruiz-Geli, Cloud 9

Media Tic Building, Barcelona

Enric Ruiz-Geli, Cloud 9

Media Tic Building, Barcelona

Enric Ruiz-Geli, Cloud 9

Media Tic Building, Barcelona

SANAA
Bright golden colour

SANAA teamed up with New York fashion designer Derek Lam and his partner Ryue Nishizawa to create a flagship store located in the heart of New York's SoHo neighbourhood. The store features a primarily white interior. Like Derek Lam's fashion, the store uses simple but refined materials such as the curving walls, made of transparent acrylic sheeting, and bright golden-coloured curtains. The designers use these walls to create what they call 'bubbles', dividing the space into smaller rooms, while keeping the space visually open. Large mirrors and simple mannequins are accompanied by custom-designed furniture.

SANAA

Derek Lam Store, New York

SANAA

Derek Lam Store, New York

SANAA

Derek Lam Store, New York

Derek Lam Store, New York

About the authors

Cees W. de Jong

Designer, author and curator. Graduated from the Gerrit Rietveld Academy,

Amsterdam. Specialist in books and exhibitions on design, typography

and architecture.

Architectural Competitions. Volume 1: 1792 – 1949. Volume 2:

1950 – today. Cees W. de Jong, Erik Mattie. Taschen, Cologne 1994.

International Book Award, AIA, American Institute of Architects, 1995.

Exhibitions: *Golden Age – 100 years of Dutch Graphic Design.* Curated

by Cees W. de Jong and Alston W. Purvis in cooperation with Premsela,

the Netherlands Institute for Design and Fashion. The exhibition was

presented and organised by Cees W. de Jong in Bucharest, Sophia,

Budapest, Madrid, Breda, Ljubljana, Istanbul, Brno and Athens 2008-2010.

Type. A Visual History of Typefaces and Graphic Styles. Published in

6 languages. Volume 1: 1628 – 1900. Volume 2: 1900 – 1939. Cees W. de

Jong, Alston W. Purvis and Jan Tholenaar. Taschen, Cologne. Hardcover

edition 2009, 2010. Paperback edition, two volumes in a slipcase 2012.

Design and layout: *Megg's History of Graphic Design* 5th edition.

Philip B. Meggs, Alston W. Purvis. John Wiley and Sons, Hoboken 2011.

Design and international co-publishing: *The Book of Books. 500 Years of*

Graphic Innovation. University of Amsterdam. Special Collections Library.

Thames & Hudson, London. DuMont Buchverlag, Cologne. Amsterdam

University Press, Amsterdam. Uitgeverij Lannoo, Tielt 2012 – 2013.

São Paulo State University Press, São Paulo. Pyramyd Éditions, Paris.

Guangzhou Shengya Culture Communication, Guangzhou, China.

Erik Mattie

Studied Art History and Archaeology, and Dutch Law in Amsterdam.

Mattie writes for publications on a regular basis on the subjects of architec-

ture and urbanism. Together with Cees W. de Jong, he published the prize-

winning book *Architectural Competitions*, which was awarded the best

architectural historical book of 1995 by a jury of the American Institute of

Architects. In 1999, Erik Mattie became the director of *M&DM*, founded in

1995, one of the oldest consulting agencies in the Netherlands undertak-

ing researching and consulting on architecture, urbanism and heritage.

Bert de Muynck

Architect, writer and co-director of *MovingCities*. In September 2011,

Bert de Muynck took up a position as Assistant Professor at the University of

Hong Kong Faculty of Architecture based at the HKU Shanghai Study Center.

MovingCities is a Shanghai-based think-tank investigating the role that

architecture and urbanism play in shaping the contemporary city. Established

in Beijing in 2007 by Bert de Muynck and Mónica Carriço, *MovingCities* has

conducted research, lectures, creative consultancy and workshops in China,

Israel, Sweden, Netherlands, Finland, Italy and Indonesia. In 2014, *Moving-*

Cities and Professor Marino Folin curated *Adaptation – Architecture and Change*

in China, a collateral exhibition of the 2014 Venice Architecture Biennale.

Sophie Roulet

Architect (DPLG, France), designer (ENSD) and journalist. Since 1996 she has

been responsible for news on architecture and design at the architecture

journal *Archicréé* and works in Paris as the permanent correspondent

of the magazine *A 10: new European architecture.* She is the author or editor of various publications on architecture including *Toyo Ito. Collections Monographie d'Architecte* (1991) and *Piscines. Collections Monographie d'Architecte* (1992) published by Édition du Moniteur and *Design et Games. Les Villages* (2001, with CNAP and Michel Bavery Editeur) and *Le Design dans les collections du Fonds national d'art contemporain* (2002) published by Éditions Hazan. In addition, she has curated a number of exhibitions in collaboration with MOSTRA, including *60 ans de logement social 1944 – 2004. Le Ministère de l'Equipement* (Jardin des Tuileries, 2004), *Montagnes célestes, Trésors des musées de Chine* (Galeries Nationales du Grand Palais, 2004), *La DS a cinquante ans* (Cité des Sciences et de l'Industrie, 2005), *Exposition Permanente des Globes de Coronelli à la BNF* (Hall de la Bibliothèque Nationale de France, 2006), *Pharaon: Homme, Roi, Dieu* (Musée des Beaux-Arts de Valenciennes, 2007), *2 CV Expo Show* (Cité des Sciences et de l'Industrie, 2007), *La Terre et Nous* (Cité des Sciences et de l'Industrie, 2008), *Exposition De Terre et de Feu, l'aventure de la céramique européenne* (Limoges, 2010), *Pavillon Paris – Île de France* (Shanghai Expo, 2010) and *La voie du Tao: un autre chemin de l'Etre* (Grand Palais, 2010).

Acknowledgements

BIG-Bjarke Ingels Group, Copenhagen and New York

Museum of Biodiversity, Panama

Stefano Boeri Architetti, Milano

China Digital Times

Gehry Partners, LLP, Los Angeles

Zaha Hadid Architects, London

Herzog & de Meuron Architects, Basel

Steven Holl Architects, New York

Toyo Ito & Associates, Architecs, Tokyo

Lui Jiakun Architects, Chendu

Michael Malzan Architecture, Los Angeles

El Equipo de Mazzanti, Bogota

A. Victoria Murillo Istmophoto, Panama

Ateliers Jean Nouvel, Paris

Enric Ruiz-Geli, Cloud 9, Barcelona

SANAA I Kazuyo Sejima + Ryue Nishizawa, Tokyo

Wang Shu, Hangzhou

Illustration credits

Reference literature

Alessandro Mendini 30 Colours: New Colours for a new Century. V+K, Bussum / AkzoNobel, 1996.

Brand, Jan; Janselijn, Han, *Architectuur en Verbeelding: Architecture and Imagination.* Waanders, Zwolle 1989.

Desmier-Maulion, Annick, *Paris, La couleur de la ville.* Éditions de La Villette, Paris 2002.

Jodidio, Philip, *Contemporary American Architects.* Taschen Verlag, Cologne 1993.

Jodidio, Philip, *New Forms: Architecture in the 1990s.* Taschen Verlag, Cologne 2001.

Norberg-Schulz, Christian, *Genius Loci: Towards a Phenomenology of Architecture.* Academy Editions Ltd, London 1980.

Norman Foster 30 Colours: New Colours for a new Century. V+K, Blaricum / AkzoNobel, 1998.

Papadakis, Andreas; Steele, James, *Architecture of Today*. Rizzoli Publications, New York 1997.

Pitz, Helge; Brenne, Winfried, *Die Bauwerke und Kunstdenkmäler von Berlin, Beiheft 1, Bezirk Zehlendorf. Siedlung Onkel Tom / Einfamilienreihenhäuser 1929. Architekt Bruno Taut.* Gebr. Mann Verlag, Berlin 1980.

Rem Koolhaas: OMA 30 Colours. V+K, Blaricum / AkzoNobel, 1999.

Richard Meier. Thirty Colours. V+K, Blaricum / AkzoNobel, 2003.

Taverne, Ed; Wagenaar, Cor, *The Colour of the City*. V+K, Laren 1992.

Colophon

Compiled by:

Cees W. de Jong, VK Projects, Naarden

Design and layout:

Cees W. de Jong, VK Projects, Naarden.

In collaboration with

Asher Hazelaar, Puls, Ermelo

Translation:

Textcase, Utrecht

Copy editing:

Julian Reisenberger, Weimar

Printed by:

DZS Grafik, Ljubljana